THE
BIBLICAL
BASIS
OF
MISSIONS

AVERY T. WILLIS, JR.

CONVENTION PRESS
NASHVILLE, TENNESSEE

Contents

About the Author

Avery T. Willis, Jr. is well qualified to write this text for the Baptist Doctrine Study. He is presently supervisor of the Adult section of the Church Training Department of the Sunday School Board. This places him in a position to be in touch with the training needs of adults. Dr. Willis came to his present responsibility from the mission field where he served as president of the Indonesian Baptist Theological Seminary. Consequently, he writes with the expertise of an educator and with the heart of a missionary.

A native of Arkansas, Dr. Willis is a graduate of Oklahoma Baptist University and of Southwestern Baptist Theological Seminary where he received the Th.D. degree in 1974 with a major in missions and minors in philosophy and in preaching. He pastored churches in Oklahoma and in Texas for ten years before being appointed by the Foreign Mission Board of the Southern Baptist Convention.

Three Ways to Study This Book

LARGE-GROUP STUDY
This book can be studied in a large group. These large-group sessions will be more effective if the leader will adapt the small-group study guides for use by a larger group and use the teaching aids in *The Biblical Basis of Missions Resource Kit* (item 5123-10).

SMALL-GROUP STUDY
Church Training groups or other small groups can study this book by using the directions for leading small-group sessions. These guides are in *The Biblical Basis of Missions Resource Kit.*

INDIVIDUAL STUDY
You can study this book on your own as well as in a group. Carefully work through each chapter, completing each Personal Learning Activity as it appears in the text. You will be introduced to fresh ideas. Take time to consider and to evaluate each one.

Requirements for receiving credit in the Church Study Course for the study of this book are at the end of the text. *(See table of contents.)*

Preface

A few months after I began my first pastorate, Mrs. Jefferies, a faithful but outspoken member, said, "Brother Avery, you know what I like about your preaching?" I leaned forward expectantly. "It's that you don't preach no doctrine." Stunned, I slumped back in my chair.

"But everything I preach is doctrine, Mrs. Jefferies!" I exclaimed.

"Well, it don't sound like it."

"But doctrine means truth or teaching. Everything I preach is doctrine because I preach the Bible."

From the outset, I want you to know that this book may not sound like doctrine, but it is. I encourage you to read the Word along with the book to test the truth of my interpretations. If the book causes you to examine the Word to discover for yourself the biblical basis of missions, I will have succeeded.

I do not intend for this book to sound like a theological textbook. I have studied most of the theological textbooks on missions, but I doubt that many people would read this book if it were couched in those terms or documented extensively. I have written dialogue to help some of the key issues come alive. The Scripture passages from which these truths were derived usually are listed following the accounts so that you can study the Bible for yourself and determine their validity. My primary concern is for you to see this world from God's perspective and understand his plan to establish his kingdom.

My first interest in writing this book began fifteen years ago in a missions seminar when a professor remarked that Baptists needed an up-to-date book on the biblical basis of missions. I was startled because I thought that everything on the biblical basis of missions had been written already. Ten years ago I wrote an outline and did research on the contents of this book. I realized then that I did not understand nor had I experienced all that I had discovered in the Bible about missions. I had served one term of missionary service, but I returned to Indonesia to put into practice what God had revealed to me in his Word.

Through fourteen years of missionary experiences in Indonesia, God has forced me to study his Word over and over for a deeper understanding of the biblical basis of missions and its implications for us today. He has given me a fresh perspective of his purpose and plan for the world and the ways he intends to bring people of all nations to himself. I hope that this attempt to share these insights with you will result in your understanding the biblical basis of missions; but even more, I hope that it will result in your making world missions the overriding purpose of your life.

No doubt you will read some things here that you have never heard before. I hope that you will be like the Bereans who "received the word with all readiness of mind, and searched the scriptures daily, whether those things were so" (Acts 17:11).

Acknowledgments
I want to thank Dr. Roy Edgemon and the Church Training Department of the Sunday School Board for asking me to write this book. I also want to express appreciation for the confidence of the mission agencies that recommended me as the author.

Dr. R. Cal Guy and Dr. Jack Gray of Southwestern Baptist Theological Seminary stimulated my thinking and encouraged me to study the biblical basis of missions. Many authors contributed to my thinking. A selected bibliography at the end of each chapter lists some of the books that I found helpful.

My deepest appreciation goes to my wife, Shirley, and our five children, Randal, Sherrie, Wade, Krista, and Brett, because the time used to write the book was taken from them. Shirley also typed the manuscript and made many helpful suggestions.

My missionary colleagues and my Indonesian brethren deserve recognition for their willingness to attempt to turn to a more biblical model of missions. They have been patient and supportive in attempts that succeeded and in those that failed. They taught me much.

Bill Latham, editor, and Anne Donahue, manuscript assistant, have improved the manuscript and have made it more readable.

For all of these and many more unmentioned friends who have helped me, I give glory to God. Any errors and shortcomings in the book are my own.

AVERY T. WILLIS, JR.

Introduction

Today's realities demand a new look at the biblical basis of missions. Modern missions is the fad of the few. Not since the first century has missions been given its rightful place in the ministry of the church. Of course, efforts have been made to take the gospel to the uttermost parts of the earth by churches, missions boards, societies, and individuals; but if we were to count all those involved in any phase of missions, the percentage would be dismally small.

MISCONCEPTIONS ABOUT MISSIONS

The results of the fad-of-the-few-mentality have been disastrous. Two misconceptions have been most damaging. First, missions is perceived as a super special assignment for extraordinary people. Nothing could be farther from God's purpose. The Bible teaches that God's method is to use the foolish, the weak, and the despised persons of the world to bring glory to him (1 Cor. 1:26-31). God's purpose is to be accomplished by ordinary people who believe in and serve an extraordinary God.

Paul has been upheld as the ideal missionary for so long that many fail to realize that the spread of the gospel in the first century was accomplished primarily by people named Barnabas, Silas, Mark, Aquila, Epaphroditus, and a host of other Christians. God intends to use everyone—the Marks and the Epaphrodituses, as well as the Pauls—to accomplish his mission.

If we are to carry out God's mission during our lifetime, we must erase from our minds the idea that only unusually gifted persons are missionaries. Such thinking discourages one from identifying himself with missions unless he thinks he has an extraordinary gift and calling. This kind of thinking places a halo over the missionary's head, making it impossible for him to measure up to the ideal.

A second misconception fostered by the fad-of-the-few-mentality is that world missions can be done by proxy. Some think missionaries are their substitutes in world evangelization. They feel satisfied to pray for missionaries, to support them, and to encourage them. All these things should be done, but doing them does not relieve each Christian of his responsibility to be involved directly in God's mission.

Missions by proxy is the standard operating procedure in many churches. Some leave missions to the Woman's Missionary Union and expect the women to be responsible for the church's involvement in missions. At other times the Home Mission Board and the Foreign Mission Board are expected to take full responsibility for fulfilling the mandate that God gave to all his people. Some Christians interpret their giving as *paying* their part of the Cooperative Program and thereby discharging their obligations to evangelize the world.

Missionaries, mission agencies, and mission boards are practical expressions of concern by Christians and local churches, but these alone cannot fulfill the obligation God has given to every Christian and to every church. Not everyone can be a missionary, but everyone can be on mission for God.

DEFINITION OF TERMS

Let me define some terms that will be used throughout the

book. By *mission,* I mean the total redemptive purpose of God to establish his kingdom. *Missions,* on the other hand, is the activity of God's people, the church, to proclaim and to demonstrate the kingdom of God to the world. The word *mission* comes from the Latin word *mittere* meaning *to send.* God is both the *sender* and the *sent* (in Christ). The church is *sent* by God on mission and cooperates with God *to send* missionaries. *Missionaries* are set apart by God and the church to cross natural or cultural barriers with the gospel.

I make this distinction because missions always is in danger of becoming the expression of man. Missions places the church at the center of the world's conflicts. Without a biblical base, the church will fail to be true to God's mission. Missions can become identified easily with the culture of the sender or be seduced by elements of the culture in which it is being expressed. For example, the East India Company was charged with the task of missions to Indonesia, but it subordinated missions for the benefit of its financial empire. Resurgent nationalism around the world reacts to any attempt by outsiders to reform national cultures. People of other cultures quickly point out the inconsistent failures of Western civilization. They react to our superiority complex by shouting, "Yankee, go home!" In spite of that reaction, many naive Americans believe that if modern business techniques and advertising methods were practiced, other nations would flock to Christ. It is possible to franchise hamburgers, but a Westernized packaging of the gospel is often unpalatable to people of other nations.

God's mission is the prime factor in missions. Just as the fruit is the product of the vine, so missions is the product—or result—of God's mission. The way to understand missions is to begin with the vine—the mission of God. Move from the vine to the branch—the mission of the church. Then consider the fruit—missions. All three must be based on the Bible, or missions can degenerate to shallow methodology, man-made solutions, and gains that are short-lived at best.

In the first half of this book (chaps. 1-5), you will study the mission of God and the co-mission of the church. In the second half (chaps. 6-10), you will move from that theological basis to the practical expression of the mission. The biblical basis of missions encompasses both the theological and the practical aspects. However, it is not within the compass of this book to spell out all the concrete expressions of missions.

Let me alert you to three emphases in the book that could be misunderstood if not taken in the context of the whole. First, the mission of God is viewed in the order of progressive revelation—the Father, the Son, and the Spirit. The three persons of the Godhead should not be seen as so distinct that the oneness of God is violated. The Son and the Spirit were active in creation and the Old Testament period. But they are more predominant in the New Testament. Second, the motif of conflict between the kingdom of God and the kingdom of evil runs throughout the book, but it should not be seen as dualism. God is always Lord of all. But God has limited himself in this present time to save man and to involve him in the mission of God. Third, an eschatalogical tone surfaces occasionally. My intent is not to set a timetable or to endorse a particular interpretation. However, the Bible reflects a sense of biblical urgency for those of us living in the last days which were ushered in at Pentecost and will end at Christ's return.

SYNOPSIS OF THE BOOK

The thesis of this book is that missions originates and culminates with God. Chapter 1 shows that God's mission is to restore fellowship with man and make him a partner in world redemption. Man refused to be God's partner, resulting in the conflict between God and Satan on earth. Man cooperated with Satan and delayed God's plan to have his will done on earth as it is in heaven. The remainder of the book traces the conflict between the kingdom of God and the kingdom of Satan.

Chapter 2 details the mission of God's people. God refused to be thwarted by man's sin. He raised up a people to do his will and be obedient, servant-priests to all the nations of the world. He elected Israel, made a covenant with her, and disciplined her. But again and again Israel selfishly refused to fulfill her purpose. By the close of the Old Testament man had completely failed, and it appeared that God's will would never be done on earth.

Chapter 3 describes how once again the mission became God's alone. God sent Jesus as his obedient Servant-Priest to redeem man and to form a holy kingdom of priests who would demonstrate and proclaim the good news of the kingdom. Jesus fulfilled all the intent of God for Israel by becoming the disciplined Son in the incarnation, the Suffering Servant and Priest to the nations in the crucifixion, and the King of heaven and earth in the resurrection. He chose twelve disciples to be the nucleus of his new covenant people.

Chapter 4 documents how the Father and Jesus sent the Holy Spirit to take Christ's place, and to empower, inspire, and guide his chosen people in the proclamation of the good news of the kingdom to every person on earth.

Chapter 5 portrays how the church received a co-mission role with God. Christ indwells the church so it will live by the Calvary principle of priesthood, the incarnational principle of servanthood, and the resurrection principle of sonship.

Chapter 6 explores how God accomplishes his mission by multiplying disciples in all nations.

Chapter 7 discusses how God provides equippers to prepare the people of God for the work of ministry.

Chapter 8 relates how God calls all his disciples to ministry and gives them spiritual gifts to enable them to serve in the world and extend the kingdom of God.

Chapter 9 sets forth the thesis that God intercedes in the affairs of men and nations to establish his kingdom in proportion to the intercessory prayer of his people for them.

The book culminates with the mission accomplished in chapter 10. God's mission will be accomplished when Christ delivers the kingdom up to the Father. Meanwhile, he is giving his people every chance to be partners with him in establishing the kingdom and in preparing to reign with him.

CHAPTER 1

Mission of God

*The morning after I accepted Christ as Lord and
Savior, I hurried to the homes and businesses of
all my friends to tell them the good news.
Although still a child, I attempted to preach to
anyone who would listen. My one sermon was
"Christ for the Whole Wide World," based on
John 3:16. Missions is so at the heart of God that
even a child who knows John 3:16 and has
experienced new life in Christ can grasp it.*

Why is the world in such a mess? Does God not love the world?
Does he not will to do good? Does he not have all power? In
short, why is there a need for world missions?

The majesty of God's mission lies in the answer to this
problem: Why is God's will not being done on earth as it is in
heaven? Ultimate answers are found in the nature of God, in the
nature of man, in the nature of evil, and in the nature of mission.

THE NATURE OF GOD
The dilemma related to the nature of God may be diagrammed
as follows:

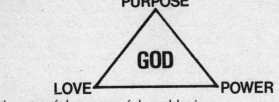

God is powerful, purposeful, and loving.

Powerful

Step on a rocket with me and catch a glimpse of the greatness of God. We travel at the speed of light, 186,282 miles per second. As we blast off, our seats afford us a clear view of earth. One second later earth has dropped away until it appears no larger than a huge balloon. In two seconds we have shot past the moon and stolen a glance at the now-famous moon shot of earth. Eight and one-half minutes later we pass the sun. Earth appears to be a speck 93 million miles away in the darkness of space.

Five hours later we leave our solar system and can no longer distinguish earth from myriads of other planets and stars. After four years of travel at the speed of light, we zip by the nearest star, Alpha Centauri. For almost 100,000 years we travel across the Milky Way, our own galaxy. After that, we travel another 1,500,000 years before we reach the Great Nebula, most distant of the six other galaxies in what astronomers call the Local Group. Up to this point we might compare our journey to a family traveling across country whose five-year-old asks before they get out of town, "How much farther is it?" In the great vastness of space, we must travel at least 4,500 *million* years at the speed of light before we begin to reach the area of the universe that cannot be seen with telescopes from our planet. And who knows how much lies beyond?

Yet Isaiah says God "hath measured the waters in the hollow of his hand, and meted out heaven with the span" (Isa. 40:12). He measures space by the width of his hand.

A vision of God's greatness must increase our wonder at his mission. "The heavens declare the glory of God" (Ps. 19:1), but only a bit of it. When we compare God's infiniteness with our limitations of time and space, we say with the psalmist, "When I consider thy heavens, the work of thy fingers, the moon and the stars, which thou hast ordained; what is man, that thou art mindful of him? and the son of man, that thou visitest him?" (Ps. 8:3-4).

Certainly the world's mess is not caused by any lack of power and greatness on God's part.

Loving

To understand God better, we must reverse our rocket and return to earth for the psalmist asserts, "For thou hast made him a little lower than the angels, and hast crowned him with glory and honour. Thou madest him to have dominion over the works of thy hands; thou hast put all things under his feet" (Ps. 8:5-6).

God loves man. Can you imagine the great God who created all the universe visiting earth, forming man out of dust, and breathing life into him (Gen. 2:7)? As the crown of God's creation, man was placed in a perfect environment that provided everything he needed (Gen. 2:8-14). God even created woman as a loving companion who perfectly complemented him (Gen. 2:18). God communed with the finite creature that he had made in his image. He entrusted man with his creation and gave him dominion over it. God's provision, fellowship, and trust prove God's love. It is not because of God's lack of love that the world is in such trouble.

Purposeful

One quick look at the created order convinces us that God is a god of purpose.

> For all God's words are right, and everything he does is worthy of our trust. He loves whatever is just and good; the earth is filled with his tender love. He merely spoke, and the heavens were formed, and all the galaxies of stars. And with a breath he can scatter the plans of all the nations who oppose him, but his own plan stands forever (Ps. 33:4-6,10-11, TLB).

The patterns God has placed in the building blocks of the universe make it possible for science to exist. Without the consistency of those patterns, scientists could never verify an experiment because they could not be sure that the elements would react the same way under the same conditions. The astronomer can predict precisely the location and movement of the stars and planets because they were made according to the purpose of God. "The heavens declare the glory of God; and the firmament sheweth his handiwork" (Ps. 19:1).

From our vantage point today we do not understand all the original purpose of God in creation, but we do know that it was good. We know that man was to be a partner in its development and that God and man communed regularly about it. In the opening chapters of the Bible, we glimpse the nature of God as powerful, purposeful, and loving, and we begin to understand his mission. Certainly, there was no lack in God's original purpose that caused the malfunction that we experience in the world today.

Why then does God allow the world to exist as it is? Certainly, it could not be that he does not love man, for he spared not his own Son to save man (Rom. 8:32). It is not because of God's will that things are not better, for God is not willing that any should perish (2 Pet. 3:9). Neither is it a lack of power, for God himself says, "Behold, I am the Lord, the God of all flesh: is there any thing too hard for me?" (Jer. 32:27).

Since God loves us and is powerful enough to do whatever he pleases, the answer must lie somewhere in his will; and that involves the nature of man.

PERSONAL LEARNING ACTIVITY 1
List three qualities of God's nature from which mission flows.

THE NATURE OF MAN

The nature of man adds another dimension to the mission of God and explains part of the dilemma. God created man in his own image, which meant that man was good, responsible, and capable of communion with God (Gen. 1:27). But he created man from dust, which meant that man was finite and limited to time and space (Gen. 2:7).

Man's ability to think, to will, and to feel reflect the image of God. But the likeness of God was most evident in man's moral nature.

Relational

Because man reflected God's image, his primary need was relational. Man desired relationships with God and other created beings to experience wholeness.

Man discovered his true nature and identity in his face-to-face relationship with God and in his relationship to creation. He knew he was different from other created beings. He could think, talk, and interact with creation in ways animals could not. More important, he found he could communicate with God.

However, as man related to God, he became aware that God was the Other—different from man or creation. God was infinite; man was finite. God had unlimited power; man's was limited. God could be anywhere; man could be only one place at a time. God knew all things; man was still learning. God was independent; man was dependent. God was Spirit; man was flesh as well as spirit. In this relationship man was secure. God loved man, and man responded. God trusted him, and man trusted God. His awareness of his identity made him at home with God and with the world. He worshiped God and was happy to be his friend.

Responsible

God made man responsible by giving him dominion over all living beings on the earth. Original man must have had great intellectual powers to know and name all the animals (Gen. 2:19-20). We do not know how man ruled over the domain God had created for him, but it is clear that he was to be responsible for it.

Man's second responsibility was to subdue the earth. He had the right to master his material environment and to make it serve him. God placed man in Eden and told him "to dress it and to keep it" (Gen. 2:15).

Man's third responsibility was to "be fruitful, and multiply, and replenish the earth" (Gen. 1:28). He was responsible for his descendants.

Finite

Man's finiteness was not evil but, instead, the strongest reason for dependence on God. Although man had limitations, he had every power he needed to live a happy life. His susceptibility to death emerged only after he overstepped his dominion.

Man rebelled against his dependence on God and enthroned self. He desired to "be as gods, knowing good and evil" (Gen. 3:5). Man's nature was corrupted. In one stroke he sacrificed his close relationship with God, his cooperative relationship with the created order, and became subject to sin and death (Gen. 3:16-24).

Man lost his self-identity in the Fall because he was no longer properly related to the Other. His lack of wholeness caused him to relate improperly to his fellowman. He sought identity and security by comparing himself to others whom he considered inferior or by becoming hostile to those he perceived as superior. He created a fractured society that sustains itself by making distinctions of race, class, intellect, prowess, religion, and so forth.

Therefore, man is alienated from God, dislocated from his original position in the created order, and estranged from his fellowman.

Concurrently with man's sin and evil, there developed a destructive fault in the created order. Paul described man's fallen condition in a fallen world: "For we know that the whole creation groaneth and travaileth in pain together until now. And not only they, but ourselves also, which have the firstfruits of the Spirit, even we ourselves groan within ourselves, waiting for the adoption, to wit, the redemption of our body" (Rom. 8:22-23).

Part of the dilemma mentioned above begins to clear. In giving man freedom, God had limited himself to some degree. He gave man the responsibility of choice and let him suffer the consequences of his wrong choices.

Another aspect of God's nature emerges—his righteousness and justice. He punished man and the serpent. But because he loved man, he did not give up on him. God's mission is to

sin = human limitation

agapo

restore man to wholeness so he can be related properly to God, man, and the created order.

God's mission not only flows from his own nature but flows toward man's fallen nature to restore a right relationship between himself and man.

PERSONAL LEARNING ACTIVITY 2
Write a paragraph in your own words about how the nature of man complicated God's mission.

---

hamartia - missing the mark; limited

THE NATURE OF EVIL

Another factor complicated God's mission—Satan usurped authority. Before Satan entered the picture, there was no sin, sickness, death, war, or discord on earth. Man lived in a perfect environment created by a loving, personal, purposeful God. But when man yielded to the temptation of the serpent, he loosed an evil power in the earth.

In essence man traded lords. He surrendered to Satan his God-given right to dominion over the earth. Although man surrendered his dominion, he did not surrender earth's ownership. The earth is still God's. But now it has a new master. Satan and his evil spirits have set up residence on the earth and oppose God and his kingdom. *Luke 10:18*

Satan's origin is unclear; but whenever he comes on the scene, he tries to usurp power over man and the world. The Bible says that he is the prince of this world (John 14:30; 16:11), and the god of this world (2 Cor. 4:4). As prince of the power of the air (Eph. 2:2), he heads a vast horde of demons, principalities, powers, rulers of the darkness of this world, and wicked hosts of the spirit world (Eph. 6:11). He claims to have authority over all the kingdoms of this world (Matt. 4:1-11). John said, "We know that we are of God, and the whole world lies in the power of the evil one" (1 John 5:19, NASB).

The nature of evil necessitates God's judgment. Man who becomes a part of the kingdom of evil by his sin must also be

teleios - maturity, effectiveness, perfection

punished. God's mission, however, is to redeem man from the clutches of evil and save him.

So often we are oblivious to the malevolent power of evil that pervades the world. We seem not to realize that it is robbing God of glory and man of salvation. Throughout this book references will be made to Satan and the forces of evil. God is much greater than Satan (1 John 4:4); but in the present conflict on earth, God has chosen to involve man through his love and his purpose in overcoming the Evil One.

Now we come to a key part of the answer to the world's dilemma. God is powerful enough to create again a perfect world. He loves man and is willing to do whatever is necessary to save him. However, God's moral nature requires that he punish sin and rebellion. Then why doesn't he do it and get it over?

In God's infinite wisdom he purposely has limited himself to some extent by the kind of relationship he desires with man. He created man free and responsible. God will not violate that relationship even if man does. Therefore, God works through all things to lead man again to enthrone God as Lord, and to do it of

his own free will. God works through man to reestablish his kingdom. Man cannot bring the kingdom, but he can recognize it and become a partner with God. God does not want a kingdom of slaves but of free men who joyfully and willingly worship him.

Given the nature of God, the nature of man, and the nature of evil, the world's dilemma will not be solved until God's mission is accomplished.

THE NATURE OF THE MISSION *Mark 16:15*

Missions originated in the heart of God. It is not something we decide to do for God, but God reveals his purpose to us so that we may have a creative part in his mission. Make no mistake, we do not initiate the mission nor will we consummate it. But somehow, some way, and to some extent, God has limited what he will do. That limit is the possibility of what he can do through us (Ps. 78:41). God sums up our awesome responsibility and the faith he puts in us in three basic purposes of his mission and ours.

To Bring Glory to God ←

In the letter to the Ephesians, Paul stated three times that God's eternal plan is for his people to be to the praise of his glory (Eph. 1:6,12,14). Throughout the chapter, God stands as both the originator and the goal of the redemptive process. Scholars agree that the glory of God is the ultimate goal of God's mission.

God receives glory when man fully realizes the purpose of his existence, consciously praises God for his grace, and joyfully demonstrates God's grace by being filled with all the fullness of God (Eph. 3:19).

> The goal which one envisions is of such great importance for the mission because one's conception of the goal determines to a great extent one's motive for participation in the mission. . . . Those, therefore, who find in God final goal are impelled to conscious mission by the most urgent and compelling motivation possible. These cannot rest until all men praise God, until

every tongue confesses the Christ, until every knee bows before him, and until all the ends of the earth have been reached with the gospel of Jesus. For these are conscious that while there is one tongue yet silent, or one knee still unbent, God is not receiving the glory due unto him in and from his creation.[1]

To Share the Good News with the Alienated ←

God's mission includes recreating man spiritually. "We are his workmanship, created in Christ Jesus unto good works, which God hath before ordained that we should walk in them" (Eph. 2:10). God restores man's identity and his purpose for being.

At the same time God creates a new society without barriers (Eph. 2:13-22). The mystery of God's mission is clear: "That the Gentiles should be fellow-heirs, and of the same body and partakers of his promise" (Eph. 3:6). He has entrusted his people with the mission expressed by Paul: "Unto me, who am less than the least of all saints, is this grace given, that I should preach among the Gentiles the unsearchable riches of Christ; and to make all men see what is the fellowship of the mystery, which from the beginning of the world hath been hid in God, who created all things by Jesus Christ" (Eph. 3:8-9).

To Display the Wisdom of God to Evil Powers ←

In some way yet unrevealed, man becomes God's display of his wisdom to Satan and his evil beings: "In order that the manifold wisdom of God might now be made known through the church to the rulers and the authorities in the heavenly places" (Eph. 3:10, NASB). Redeemed man is the primary exhibit of God's grace. We are not informed about all the conflict between the two kingdoms although we are obviously in the midst of the struggle. Nevertheless, God seems to be depending on us to demonstrate his goodness, wisdom, and power. We do not understand what is at stake for God, but we are told that it is supremely important to him and to us.

Each of us feels uncertain about his purpose in life until God reveals it to him. One purpose of this book is to help you realize how important you, as an individual, and the church, as the people of God, are to God.

PERSONAL LEARNING ACTIVITY 3
List three purposes of God's mission.

God intends for man to bring glory to him, to share the good news with the alienated, and to display God's wisdom to evil powers.

God is determined to accomplish his mission on his terms. He will not coerce man, nor will he be coerced by man. Rather, he will lead man by love. After man fell, he continued to disappoint God. He became so wicked that "every imagination of the thoughts of his heart was only evil continually. And it repented the Lord that he had made man on the earth, and it grieved him at his heart" (Gen. 6:5-6). *naham - grieved went had pity on man.*

PERSONAL LEARNING ACTIVITY 4
Write in your own words what you think it meant for God to repent and be grieved (Gen. 6:6-7). Then think of the deepest hurt you have ever experienced. Write three or four words describing how you felt. Now try to imagine how God feels about man's failure to do his will.

It is difficult to understand the meaning of the words "It repented the Lord." To repent means to change one's mind, action, or behavior. Sometimes the truth that God is unchanging is interpreted to mean that he is static, not active, and is not affected by anything man does. But when the Bible says God is unchanging, it means he is unchanging in his character.

Although God destroyed most of the people he created, his mercy caused him to stop before he destroyed them all. So, although God was "sorry" for the way man had corrupted all his creation, he did not "repent" in the sense that he reversed his previous purpose. He maintained his purpose but redirected his plan to accomplish it.

The writers of the Bible were incapable of expressing God's feelings in other than human terms. Make no mistake; God has emotions. Emotions are one part of God's image that was placed in man. Most of us in the Western world have been influenced unconsciously by the idea of Greek philosophy that God is the Unmoved Mover who stoically sits on a throne without acting or feeling. Even a surface study of the Bible will reveal that God is grieved, hurt, and brokenhearted over man's rebellion. He is the God who feels and acts.

No wonder the Perfect One is grieved when man willfully sins. Man tries to be like God but for the wrong reasons. He wants God's knowledge for selfish ends. He wants to rule the world as a manifestation of his own power rather than as an extension of God's authority. He wants fellowship with God based on his own works instead of on God's grace. He wants to have spiritual communion, but he has chosen to communicate with Satan and the rulers of wickedness rather than with God. He has taken God's gifts and has used them selfishly. He has become so perverted through his rebellion that he thinks that wickedness is better than righteousness. Man's rebellion and wickedness are the burden of the Lord. The Lord expresses his burden, "What iniquity have your fathers found in me, that they are gone far from me, and have walked after vanity, and are become vain?" (Jer. 2:5).

The remainder of the Bible following the Fall is the story of God's determination to reverse history and to establish his kingdom. God began again and again but each time with a marred man. Nevertheless, God has never given up on man or on his own plan to establish a kingdom of men from all nations.

Jesus later echoed this desire in Matthew 28:19 when he said, "Go ye therefore, and teach all nations." The Spirit demonstrated God's desire to reach men of all nations when, at Pentecost, men from many nations heard in their own languages about the wonderful works of God (Acts 2:11). John prophesied in the Revelation that "they sang a new song, saying, Thou . . . hast redeemed us to God by thy blood out of every kindred, and tongue, and people, and nation; and hast made us unto our God kings and priests: and we shall reign on the earth" (5:9-10).

Between Genesis 3:15, when God promised that the son of Adam would bruise the serpent's head, and Revelation 20, when Satan is cast into hell, lies the drama of the mission of God.

NOTE
1. Edwin D. Roels, *God's Mission* (Grand Rapids: William B. Eerdmans Publishing Company, 1962), p. 80.

BIBLIOGRAPHY
Carver, W. O. *Missions in the Plan of the Ages*. Nashville: Broadman Press, 1909.
Farley, Gary. *The Doctrine of God*. Nashville: Convention Press, 1977.
Vicedom, George. *The Mission of God*. St. Louis: Concordia Publishing House, 1965.

CHAPTER 2

Mission of God's People

"How odd of God to choose the Jews" was echoing in my head when I awoke in a hospital bed in Bangkok, Thailand. Evidently, while jogging that morning, I had been struck by a vehicle and had hit my head on a curb. When I came to several hours later in the hospital, not knowing where I was or what had happened, that rhythmic refrain kept reverberating through my head, "How odd of God to choose the Jews."

It does seem odd for God to choose the Jews, or anyone else, as his partners in world redemption. Why, oh, why did God limit himself to establishing his kingdom through the voluntary cooperation of man? As sovereign Lord he created the vast universe with its whirling galaxies of billions of stars. He stooped down on a small planet in a medium-sized solar system, breathed life into a mound of dust he had gathered, and called it "man."

God could have controlled all man's actions, but he chose to make him free to do good or to do evil. Man abused his freedom and disobeyed God. Relationship and fellowship with God were broken, and Adam's descendants marched resolutely away from God.

No doubt Satan and his cohorts danced with glee each time man failed. They thought the battle was won at Eden. Then at the Flood. Then at Babel. Each time, however, God found a way to continue his purpose. But after Babel when he was forced to divide man into races and scatter them over the face of the earth, it appeared God was out of options. What would he do now?

Consider the question, If I had been God, what would I have done? Check the option below that is closest to the way you feel.

_____ 1. Destroy man and forget it all. Who needs him?

_____ 2. Scatter man and let sin destroy him.

_____ 3. Start over with a man who is incapable of sin.

_____ 4. Take the risk of continuing with the original plan of complete freedom of choice for man.

_____ 5. Modify the original plan so that man can be directed through subconscious mind control.

God continued with his original plan. But he needed a new strategy. How could he get man to be a full partner voluntarily in establishing the heavenly kingdom on earth?

GOD'S ELECTION OF A PEOPLE

God's new strategy was to select <u>one individual</u> as his friend and partner. From all possible options, God elected Abraham and his descendants as the key to establishing his kingdom throughout the earth. It is odd that God would choose one person or people as his representatives on earth, but this special relationship required a special response and responsibility. God's relationship with Abraham marks a new era.

PERSONAL LEARNING ACTIVITY 6
Read in Genesis 12:1-3 the encounter God had with Abraham.[1] Answer the following questions as you discern the special ingredients in this relationship.

1. How did God get Abraham's attention? _____

   _____

2. What trait did Abraham have to exercise to obey God's command? _____

3. What inducement to obedience did God give to Abraham? _____

   _____

4. What was God's purpose in calling Abraham? _____

   _____

After you have answered these questions to your own satisfaction, read on.

God got Abraham's attention by calling him and commanding him to leave his father's house, his relatives, and his country. Abraham exercised faith because he believed the promises of God. God's inducement was a vision of being a blessing to all nations. God involved man in his purpose by forming a partnership with Abraham through election, covenant, and the response of faith.

The conflict between God's unchanging purpose and man's changing will shaped succeeding history. The key to understanding the Bible and what God is doing in this age is this—man is free to do as he wills, but God works in all situations to lead men toward God's ultimate purpose (Rom. 8:28).

An illustration of this is God's dealing with Israel. The descendants of Abraham had lost most of the sense of calling that Abraham had. It was during the Exodus event that Israel became conscious of her election. God's miraculous acts during the Exodus revealed that God actually had intervened and had acted in history. For the first time God's Chosen People knew that history was moving toward a goal instead of in endless cycles as their pagan neighbors believed. The Bible is an account of the acts of God for and through his Chosen People and therefore was written only after the Exodus.

God reveals himself by his acts. The Creation, the Flood, and the confusion of tongues at Babel helped early man know that God was powerful, righteous, and involved with man's daily life. Israel became aware of her chosen status because she experienced God acting in her behalf.

Genesis 12:1-3 is pivotal to an understanding of God's plan. He chose Abraham in order to bless all the families of the earth. When God chose Abraham, he was on his way to the world. Every person in God's election chain is a link to the rest of the world. Even when they forgot, God did not.

The Hebrew word for election-love (*ahabah*) means unconditioned love. The Old Testament writers agree that God's love, not Israel's faithfulness, was the reason for her election (Deut. 9:4-5; 7:7-8; Hos. 11:1-3; Jer. 3:4; Ex. 16:6). We do not elect God; he elects us. Election is God's initiative. The Hebrew word for election (*bahar*) means "God decides on means and ways of choosing from what is possible."[2] God makes the choice, and we have no right to question it (Rom. 9:8-24).

The question should not be, Why did God choose the Jews or us? but, For what purpose did he choose us? As a boy, I liked to play baseball. The two biggest boys automatically became captains. After tossing the bat to determine who got first choice, the captains would choose teams. When I first began to play, I was always chosen last. I was thrilled even to play. But I shall never forget the day I was chosen first. I proudly stood beside my captain and beamed as he chose the rest of the team. Many years passed before I realized that the captain had chosen me not because he liked me better than the other boys but because he felt I could help his team win the game. God's election is like that.

When God's election acts are misinterpreted, his chosen people miss their designated purpose. For example, the extreme Calvinistic interpretation of predestination has resulted in many people's interpreting election as God's decision to favor some and to damn others. The fact is that the saved are elected to help bring the lost to a knowledge to God. The Calvinistic doctrine became antimissionary when its followers said, "If God wants to save the heathen, he can do it without us." This same feeling of superiority plagued Israel and prevented God's missionary purpose from being fulfilled through them.

Have you viewed your salvation as favoritism or as a call to be involved in God's establishing his kingdom on earth? We are elected as responsible partners of God to help win the victory over Satan.

Missions is God's choice. Missionaries go at the command of the sovereign Lord, not because of their own whims or desires. No one becomes a volunteer before God elects him. This does not limit the number of missionaries. In fact, it opens the way for all God's people to be on mission. God elected a missionary people when he elected Abraham and then Israel, and then Israel's spiritual heirs.

GOD'S COVENANT WITH HIS PEOPLE

Election is not enough; man must respond. God illustrated his relationship with Israel as a marriage. Election is God's proposal. Marriage occurs only when the second party accepts the terms

33

of the proposal. As marriage is the consummation of proposed love, so the covenant was the consummation of election.

Recall that the Hebrew word for election-love (*ahabah*) means that it is an unconditioned love. The Hebrew uses a different word for covenant-love (*chesed*). It is a word that means no covenant exists until both parties meet the conditions. God's election choice was not based on Israel's goodness; however, the continuing relationship depended on their faithfulness to the covenant. God's covenant and man's response of faith initiated a new relationship between God and man. They were bound together in the common purpose of blessing all the families of the earth.

Immediately after Israel was elected out of Egypt, God took them to Sinai to reaffirm the covenant he had made with Abraham.

PERSONAL LEARNING ACTIVITY 7
Read Exodus 19:4-6. Write in your own words the conditions of God's covenant and the promises he made to Israel prior to the giving of the Ten Commandments.

The covenant proves that election is for service. God reminded Israel that he delivered them from Egypt so they would be a nation of priests to the world. Israel did not always acknowledge that God's call was for service. She certainly did not serve the nations. From generation to generation, God tried to mold his people into a nation of servant-priests.

God's pattern for making man his partner in world redemption is clear: election, covenant, and man's responsible obedience by faith. When man fails to respond, God remains faithful to his promise and purpose. He uses man's disobedience and Satan's craftiness to bring praise to his name.

God accomplishes his purpose in spite of man's sinfulness. At times man willingly follows God's commands. At other times he willfully refuses to do God's will. Israel sorely tried God's patience and purpose. But God faithfully ordered events to call her to repentance and faith.

34

PERSONAL LEARNING ACTIVITY 8

Read the following illustrations and write a paragraph explaining how God eventually works all things together to accomplish his purpose in spite of man's disobedience.

1. Abraham forsakes the Promised Land and lies about his wife (Gen. 12:10-20).
2. Abraham fails to believe God for the promised descendants (Gen. 16:1-3).
3. Jacob schemes and cheats to gain first place in the line of Abraham's descendants (Gen. 27:36).
4. Joseph is sold by his evil brothers into slavery in Egypt (Gen. 45:4-8; 50:20).
5. Moses tries to deliver Israel by his own power and plans (Ex. 2:11-15).
6. Israel refuses to enter the Promised Land according to God's time schedule (Num. 14:1-10).

You, as a Christian, are elected in Christ and inherit the promises (Gal. 3:13-16). God has called you and selected you to be one of his children. He expects you to walk in obedience to his commands and to serve him through serving the world. He is not content to have only a few select leaders but desires an entire people to be his holy servant-priests to the world.

When he saves us, God places in our hearts a desire to serve. A small-town church in Tennessee conducted a survey asking how many of its members would like to be engaged in some special service for God. Of 204 who responded to the survey, 196 said they wanted to be involved in service. They did not mean they wanted to be pastors but that they believed God had something special for them to do. Often God's people have a desire to serve but do not know what they ought to do or how to do it.

GOD'S ROLE FOR HIS PEOPLE

God intends for his people to be a disciplined people, holy

priests, and suffering servants to the world. Both the Old and New Testaments emphasize that God is forming a holy nation of servant-priests.

A Disciplined People

The Old Testament sketches God's efforts to form a holy people. Holy means to be separated unto God. God called Abraham to leave home and family and live a life of loneliness. His descendants became a pilgrim people. Israel's history is a saga of God's efforts to keep her true to her distinctive calling instead of her drifting in the direction of other peoples. She was to represent God's holiness to the other nations of the world. She soon learned that the righteousness of God demanded a disciplined, obedient people. Since God's righteousness brings his wrath upon sinners, Israel was to be a parable and a proclaimer of God's holiness.

PERSONAL LEARNING ACTIVITY 9
To understand God's intent, read Deuteronomy 7:6-11 and list the who, what, why, and how of God's relationship with his people.

Because they were his children, God had both the right and the obligation to discipline Israel. This discipline involved nurture for motivation, training for obedience, and punishment for correction in righteousness. How often God despaired at the refusal of his people to become his holy possession and fulfill his will! And he punished them each time.

More than anything else, God wanted to rule his people in righteousness. Soon after they arrived in the Promised Land, the children of Israel forgot their covenant with God to be a holy, separate nation. They demanded, "Make us a king to judge us like all the nations" (1 Sam. 8:5). An unhappy Samuel prayed to God, who answered, "They have not rejected thee, but they have rejected me, that I should not reign over them" (1 Sam. 8:7). Israel's desire to be like other nations caused them to reject God's rule over them and to subject themselves to an earthly king.

Even this extreme act of defiance did not thwart God's purpose ultimately. God changed his strategy again, this time to work through the king. After Saul, he chose David, a man after his own heart, and made a covenant to establish his kingdom forever.

Israel mistook God's blessings for his approval and thought her kingdom was synonymous with God's kingdom. She saw herself as a reservoir of God's grace to which the rest of the world must come. Her mistake was basically the same as the mistake God's people make today. We seem to think the world must come to us rather than our proclaiming the kingdom of God to the world.

Because Israel failed to understand her role in establishing God's kingdom, God destroyed her earthly power. He sent prophets to proclaim her decline and fall because she interpreted election as privilege rather than as service. God refused to allow a warped concept of his election to survive indefinitely.

The Exile in Babylon was a seventy-year object lesson to teach Israel that God alone was God and that she must obey his Law. She learned to obey the Law but failed to understand the larger lesson that she was to be a disciplined, holy people to be a blessing to others. By the beginning of New Testament times over four hundred years later, the Law itself was hardened into a legalistic mold, and the idea of Israel as God's favored people had emerged in great force. Other nations were not allowed to worship God unless they became Jews.

The purpose of discipline is to make one responsible. Israel perverted her responsibility for the nations by concentrating on herself. To be holy and separate does not mean a lack of love and contact with others. God, the most holy and separate one, is the most concerned for all people.

According to the Old Testament prophets, the hope of the kingdom would be a faithful remnant, cleansed in fiery judgment and made amenable to God's purpose. The hope was not the remnant of an earthly kingdom but the beginning of an eternal one composed of obedient children of the king.

PERSONAL LEARNING ACTIVITY 10
Read Exodus 19:3-7 and Isaiah 61:4-6. Answer in your own words the question, What did God mean when he said Israel would be a nation of priests?

A Nation of Priests

At the beginning of the covenant with Israel, God promised that they would be a kingdom of priests. Again at the close of the age, God has decreed that they shall be called "priests of the Lord" and "ministers of our God." God never wavered in his purpose (2 Pet. 2:9-11; Rev. 1:6).

God chose the tribe of Levi to be priests. They were to be models of what the whole nation was to become. The Old Testament priests brought the nation of Israel before God to worship and to learn about his holiness. Although priests had many duties, they had two main functions. First, they represented God to man. Second, they represented man to God. God intended Israel to perform these same two functions in relation to the nations.

If the entire nation was to function as priests, to whom would they be priests? Certainly not to themselves only but also to the nations. Goerner says:

> They were to become a holy priest nation to whom God
> would reveal himself that they, in turn, might transmit
> the revelation to the other nations (for all the nations
> belonged to God). They were to perform the sacrifices
> and render the service on behalf of all nations which
> would make possible God's mercy and propitiousness
> toward all.[3]

God's intention in retrospect seems clear and obvious to us; but Israel misunderstood, misinterpreted, and rejected it. God did not intend for the Israelites at this stage to take the initiative in converting the nations to God but to be faithful and to become his people. When the right time came, they were to proclaim salvation to the whole world.

A Servant People

The Lord of heaven and earth serves us and expects us to be a servant people. We are to love like God, serve like God, and minister to all people like God. The four servant passages of Isaiah clearly express the servant role of Israel and ultimately of Christ.

PERSONAL LEARNING ACTIVITY 11
Read Isaiah 42:1-7 and 49:1-12, the first two servant passages. Underline or list ideas relating the servant to the nations.

The first servant passage (Isa. 42:1-7) states that the servant will bring justice to the nations (v. 1), that the isles wait for his law (v. 4), and that the Lord will give the servant "for a covenant of the people, for a light of the Gentiles" (v. 6).

The second servant passage (Isa. 49:1-12) alerts the isles that God has called Israel. To Israel he says, "Thou art my servant, O Israel, in whom I will be glorified" (v. 3). God says that it is too light a thing to raise up the tribe of Jacob for its sake alone because, "I will also give thee for a light to the Gentiles, that thou mayest be my salvation unto the end of the earth" (v. 6). As a result kings shall arise and princes shall worship God (v. 7), and the servant will be a covenant to the people to establish the earth and inherit the people of it (v. 8).

PERSONAL LEARNING ACTIVITY 12
Read Isaiah 50:4-11 and 52:13 to 53:12, the second two servant passages, and answer the question: What is the primary requirement of the servant for the nations?

There is no way a people can become a holy nation of servant-priests without suffering. Most Jews say these Scriptures predict the suffering that they have experienced throughout the centuries and particularly at the hands of the Nazis. Note that the servant does not suffer for his own sins but for other people's sins. Israel rejected the idea of being a suffering servant. She also totally rejected the idea of a Suffering Messiah and, by New Testament times, could not accept Jesus when he fulfilled this prophecy.

Christ embraced the role that Israel rejected. He passed it on to his people as a prescribed experience. God's people must be willing to suffer if they are to be links to bring men to God. To reject the role of a suffering servant is to reject the destiny of bringing salvation to the nations.

PERSONAL LEARNING ACTIVITY 13
Compare Israel's refusal to be the kind of people God wanted with the response the people of God are making today in the following respects.

Old Testament	Today
1. An obedient people	Isaiah 11:9
2. A holy people	Isaiah 2:2
3. A disciplined people	Psalm 96:3
4. A priestly people	Psalm 68:31
5. A servant people	Psalm 22:27
6. A missionary people	Psalm 2:8

CONCLUSION

A serious question has been raised as to whether missions is taught in the Old Testament. Missions, in the sense of God's chosen people going out to the nations to take the message of salvation, was not practiced in the Old Testament. The best example in the Old Testament of missionary activity is Jonah's going to Nineveh. Yet Jonah, like Israel, refused to be God's chosen messenger to the nations. The conclusion of the Jonah episode leaves him pouting because God forgave the Ninevites instead of punishing them (Jonah 4:2). Jonah was more concerned about his gourd vine than about the repentance of the thousands of Nineveh.

The prophets and the psalmists spoke of the nations around Israel. They proclaimed God as the God of all the earth and pronounced his judgment on sinful nations. They usually restricted their prophecies relating to mission activity to the coming of other nations to Israel, and in particular to Jerusalem. Clearly, Israel cannot be our example of the missionary people.

However, if you look at the acts of God as revelations of his purpose, the Old Testament is intensely missionary. The entire story of the children of Israel is the story of the missionary God preparing a people to be missionaries. God is the missionary in the story of Jonah. God continually acted in Israel's history to reach beyond her racial borders. Ruth, a native of Moab, and Rahab, from heathen Jericho, are examples. The Old Testament concludes with the prophetic promises of future glory. Yet, the Chosen People failed utterly to fulfill God's purpose. The four hundred silent years between the Old Testament and the New Testament are mute testimonies that man was incapable of doing God's will and establishing his kingdom. Israel was more God's contrary people than his missionary people.

NOTES
1. For continuity I am using Abraham, the name God later gave to Abram.
2. G. Quell, "Election in the Old Testament," *Theological Dictionary of the New Testament*, Vol. 4, ed. Gerhard Kittel (Grand Rapids: William B. Eerdmans Publishing Company, 1967), p. 146.
3. Henry Cornell Goerner, *"Thus It Is Written": the Missionary Motif in the Scriptures* (Nashville: Convention Press, 1966), p. 14.

BIBLIOGRAPHY
Berkouwer, G. C. *Divine Election.* Grand Rapids: William B. Eerdmans Publishing Company, 1960.
Goerner, Cornell. *"Thus It Is Written": the Missionary Motif in the Scriptures.* Nashville: Convention Press, 1944.
Quell, G. "Election in the Old Testament." *Theological Dictionary of the New Testament*, Vol. 4. Edited by Gerhard Kittel. Grand Rapids: William B. Eerdmans Publishing Company, 1967.
Rowley, H. H. *The Biblical Doctrine of Election.* London: Lutterworth Press, 1964.
———. *Israel's Mission to the World.* London: Student Christian Movement Press, 1939.
———. *The Missionary Message of the Old Testament.* London: The Carey Press, 1944.
Wright, G. E. *God Who Acts.* Chicago: A. R. Allenson, Inc., 1952.

CHAPTER 3

Mission of Christ

"God has no wife; God has no sex; God has no son," my Moslem friend said vehemently. "But Mary was not God's wife," I explained. "The Holy Spirit caused a virgin to conceive miraculously. Actually, God became man."

He replied: "God is the all-powerful and is supremely one. He cannot be three Gods like you Christians teach. He is one. He is all-powerful. He could not become man."

So the logical mind of the Moslem reasons; it is unthinkable that God became man.

Only God could think up the incarnation. Man-made religions exalt men to the status of god; only the Bible teaches that God actually became man.

Picture God's mission in the Old Testament as an hourglass lying on its side. It begins with all mankind and continually narrows to an ever more select people until it reaches a dead end. No man fulfilled God's purpose. God himself had to break through the end of the glass and form a funnel that opened again on the other side to include all men. Jesus was God's breakthrough. He fulfilled all the purpose of God that Israel had failed to fulfill by becoming the disciplined Son in the incarnation, the Suffering Servant and High Priest in the crucifixion, and the King of heaven and earth in the resurrection.

THE INCARNATION

You probably have heard about and sung about the baby Jesus for so long that it seems normal to think of God in human form. In contrast, the person from a non-Christian background is dumbfounded by it. No other religion has dared to state so bluntly and so categorically that God became man.

To the Moslem it is absurd to think that the transcendent, all-powerful God could, or would, limit himself to become man. To the Hindu the distinctiveness of the incarnation, as a once-for-all coming of an only true God into actual history, is preposterous. The Buddhist cannot imagine God becoming man and living in the world where even to exist is evil. No wonder Jesus is the stone of stumbling to those who will not accept him as the revelation of God.

PERSONAL LEARNING ACTIVITY 14
Check each statement that you consider to be true.
_____1. The incarnation is illogical to the natural mind.
_____2. God took the risk that the Son could fail.
_____3. The incarnation proves God's commitment to man and his partnership in mission.
_____4. In the incarnation Jesus emptied himself of his power except that to be given by the Holy Spirit.
_____5. The incarnation demands that every person have a chance to hear the gospel.

The following Scriptures give insight that may help you in answering the above questions: (1) 1 Corinthians 2:14; Hebrews 2:9; (2) Hebrews 4:15; (3) John 1:15-16; (4) Philippians 2:7; and (5) 1 Timothy 1:15.

The uniqueness of the incarnation demands that every person in the world know about it. No man's life is complete until he has a real-life encounter with the God who invaded history. No person who has accepted Christ as God's Son should be satisfied until every man knows that God has visited earth to bring man into right relationship with his Creator. When God spoke at the beginning of time, the world was created; when God spoke by the Word in the incarnation, the new humanity was created. It cost God nothing to speak the world into existence, but it cost him his Son to create the new humanity. The incarnation is the good news that the kingdom of heaven has come in Christ.

In Philippians 2:7 the Greek word for "made himself of no reputation" (*kenoo*) means simply *to empty, to make void*, or *of no effect*. To be in the form of God means that he was no less God when he took the form of man. To be in the likeness of man means that he was no less man because he was God in the flesh. Jesus was not half God and half man but fully God and fully man.

We often focus on the divine signs at his birth and forget the humanness of it. We are amazed by the virgin birth; we rejoice in the angels' singing; we are awed at the star's appearing; we marvel at the Wise Men's journey and gifts. But so often we fail to realize that he was born in a stable to a woman who conceived him before she was married. Perhaps Mary on that first Christmas night thought: Is it possible that this is really the Son of God? It's been nine months since the angel spoke to me. Did I only dream it? If this is truly the Messiah, why are we in a stable? Why was no one here to help me give birth? Where is God?

"He is in your lap . . . as much as he is in heaven." How overwhelming the thought that the God who created all the universe limited himself to a human form, approximately eighteen inches long and weighing approximately seven pounds! No wonder other religions find it difficult to believe in the incarnation!

When the Bible used the graphic metaphor "he emptied himself," it expressed the completeness of Christ's self-renunciation. Much debate has centered on what it meant for Christ to empty himself. Whatever it meant, we cannot ignore the evidence of the New Testament that Jesus laid aside his advantages as God to face life as man. His identification and solidarity with man was complete.

Jesus had to grow in wisdom and in physical stature (Luke 2:52); he had to learn obedience (Heb. 5:8); he was actually hungry, thirsty, and tired; he experienced the emotions of anger and compassion; he endured pain; he had to live on the faith that he was the Son of God and constantly resort to the place of prayer to receive knowledge and wisdom from the Father. Yes, Jesus was really man.

Almost as startling as the incarnation was Jesus' becoming a servant. He served man in the most menial ways. He fulfilled the intentions of the Father as stated in the servant passages of Isaiah. The most graphic picture of his servant role was imprinted on the mind of man forever when Jesus took the towel and washed his disciples' feet. God, who became man, now stooped to serve man that man might catch the vision of serving.

During our first term of missionary service in Indonesia, we began Baptist work in Bogor, Java, and my secretary was a Moslem. Each Saturday I would read to her the sermon I had composed in Indonesian to see if it was grammatically correct and understandable. Often it was not the language but the concepts that were difficult for her to understand. One day I remarked off-handedly, "I love God."

She responded: "How do you love God? I don't love God."

"I love God because he first loved me. Why don't you love God?"

"I am afraid of him," she said. "I'm afraid of him because of my sins."

"I love God because he sent his Son to save me. If I didn't love him, I would not be in Indonesia," I replied.

"But I can't feel love toward him. How can I love him? We have no *penjelmaan.*"

"I am so glad you used that word *penjelmaan,*" I answered. "That is the Indonesian word for incarnation. Oh, . . . now I understand why you can't love God. If God had not become incarnate in Jesus Christ, we could not love him either. But since God first loved us and sent his Son, it is easy to love him in return."

THE CRUCIFIXION

The self-emptying of Christ climaxed with Gethsemane and Golgotha. Philippians 2:8 moves directly from Christ's incarnation to his crucifixion: "Being found in fashion as a man, he humbled himself, and became obedient unto death, even the death of the cross." Because he was the Suffering Servant, Jesus fulfilled the divine promise in Isaiah's prophecy. The cross was unavoidable.

The crucifixion did not catch the Father or the Son by surprise. God did not have to change his plans suddenly. Jesus, the Lamb of God, was slain before the foundation of the world (Rev. 13:8). Since he came to earth for that purpose, he resolutely directed his steps toward Calvary.

In Gethsemane the horror of death pressed upon him. As usual his only resource was the Father. He tried to enlist Peter, James, and John to pray for him, but they left him to face temptation alone. The battle of Gethsemane raged. Jesus wanted only to please the Father; but he sought a way to do it other than bearing the sin of mankind and facing death for every man.

For Jesus, the prospect of death was horrible because he fully knew its implications. Those who laugh at death, or stoically bear it, simply do not understand it. The physical anguish of crucifixion was only the beginning. Jesus faced death as the God-man. Can you imagine what it meant for the Life to die, for the Light to be enveloped in death's blackness, for him who knew no sin to become sin for man, for him who had never known separation from the Father to feel the aloneness of the forsaken? No wonder he said, "My soul is exceeding sorrowful, even unto death" (Matt. 26:38).

The battle that had raged during the wilderness temptation reached fever pitch. Satan had left him "for a season" but had assaulted him at every opportunity thereafter.

Satan entered into Peter only a short while before Gethsemane. A few moments after he had confessed that Jesus was the Christ, the Son of the living God, Peter rebuked Jesus for saying he was going to suffer and die. Jesus had to say to Peter, "Get thee behind me, Satan" (Matt. 16:23). Satan stopped short of nothing to prevent Jesus from saving man. Satan assaulted the humanity of Jesus in Gethsemane to tempt him to draw back from his impending sacrifice. The human and divine wills clashed. "Being in an agony he prayed more earnestly: and his sweat was as it were great drops of blood falling down to the ground" (Luke 22:44).

Jesus was not role-playing. The battle was real. Yet Jesus so completely surrendered to the Father that the struggle centered on knowing the Father's will. Jesus' will, always submissive to the Father's, overcame both the physical reality and Satan's demonic presence when he uttered, "Not my will, but thine, be done" (Luke 22:42). Jesus won the war of the ages at that moment! He arose with a confidence that never wavered in the face of soldiers, suffering, and death. For him, to know the Father's will was to do it. He became "obedient unto death, even the death of the cross" (Phil. 2:8).

Jesus fulfilled the priestly role by his intercessory prayers and by his death. He positioned himself between sinful man and the holy God as an intercessor. Jesus "in the days of his flesh, when he had offered up prayers and supplications with strong crying and tears unto him that was able to save him from death, . . . learned he obedience by the things which he suffered" (Heb. 5:7-8). In so doing, he became the author of salvation. The Father recognized him as High Priest after the order of Melchizedek.

Jesus, as Priest, represented man to God as well as God to man. His divinity qualified him to represent God; his humanity qualified him to represent man. By means of his death Jesus became the advocate for all men who would come to God through him.

Jesus gladly accepted the role that Israel had rejected— Priest and Suffering Servant. What a nation had refused to do and what a tribe of Levites had failed to accomplish, Jesus fulfilled. In doing so, he opened the door for every believer to become a priest.

Jesus' death was an act of atonement which in the Old Testament meant the covering of sin through God's own provision. On the basis of the atonement, Jesus reconciled man to God (2 Cor. 5:14 to 6:2).

Jesus' death not only affected man's feeling about God, it paid for man's sin in an objective, historical sense. Communion between God and man was made possible through it (Heb. 9:12, 26-28; 10:10; 1 Tim. 2:4-5).

By his death Jesus satisfied the Father, subdued Satan, and reconciled man to God. Forgiveness was made available to those who believe in Christ as Savior on the basis of his sacrifice.

Some people say that Jesus died only for those who believe in him. Others say he died for the whole world, including those who reject him. Which do you think is correct? Read John 16; 2 Corinthians 5:19; and Romans 5:8 to decide before reading further.

If you answered that Jesus died for the world, what are the implications of that truth for us who have been made ambassadors and have had committed to us the word of reconciliation? Read 2 Corinthians 5:20.

Since Christ died for the world, every man has a right to choose salvation. Man may choose not to respond to Christ's offer; but if he is not given a chance to respond, we have sinned against him. We must beseech man to be reconciled to God.

After I had talked with my secretary about the incarnation, I told her that Christ died for her.

"But he didn't die for me," she replied; "he died for Christians."

"No," I said, "he died for you. He died for everyone."

"But we do not accept him."

"Nevertheless, he died for you anyway. What a pity that you don't receive him."

"But we didn't want him to die for us," she said in exasperation.

"He still wanted to die for you because he knew that your sins could never be forgiven unless he paid the price for them on the cross. On what basis do you believe you have forgiveness?"

"I'm not sure," she replied. "We just ask God for it and do good."

"That is good," I replied, "but God cannot forgive you until there is an objective basis for that forgiveness. Someone must die for your sins. The only basis he accepts is the one that he has provided in Jesus. The Bible says, 'Neither is there salvation in any other: for there is none other name under heaven given among men, whereby we must be saved' (Acts

4:12)."

"But why did he have to die?"

"Because there was no other way for a person to be saved. If there had been any other way, Jesus would not have died. The night before the crucifixion he asked the Father if there were any other way, but there wasn't. Jesus said, 'I am the way, the truth, and the life: no man cometh unto the Father, but by me' (John 14:6)."

As the second Adam, Jesus restored what the first Adam lost. There are only two reasons men are lost: one, they have never adequately heard the message of salvation, or, two, they have rejected God's offer of reconciliation in Christ. We cannot do much about the second reason, but it is our obligation to eliminate the first reason.

After Satan's bold plan of eliminating Christ had failed, he tried a sneak attack to convince man that the redemptive acts of Christ are not necessary for salvation. Since he could not stop Christ, Satan attempts to convince men that there are other ways of salvation outside of Christ.

Paradoxically, just at the time Baptists are engaged in Bold Mission Thrust, the philosophy of the world has crept into the life-stream of our membership and sapped our spiritual strength. Thought patterns growing out of universalism, humanism, and secularism have robbed many Baptists of the verve and audacity to proclaim Jesus Christ as Savior and Lord to every person. This insidious, worldly philosophy is daily heard in expressions such as, "Other nationalities have their own religions; don't disturb them!" or, "Who are we to tell them that they are wrong if they don't accept Christ as the only way?" or, "We haven't done so well ourselves; we should clean up our own back doorstep before we go to other nations to tell them how to live." When we cease to believe that Jesus is the only way of salvation, we disqualify ourselves for God's mission.

Our task as priests is not to offer a sacrifice for sin but to proclaim the sacrifice that Jesus has made. Our priestly role is to make the cross real to people at the crossroads of their lives.

PERSONAL LEARNING ACTIVITY 16
In seventy-five words or less, compare the priestly roles of Israel, of Christ, and of the believer.

THE RESURRECTION

If a reporter had interviewed Satan while Jesus was being buried, the interview might have sounded something like this.

"Excuse me for taking you away from your celebration, but I'd like to ask you a few questions. How do you feel about the present situation now that Jesus is dead?"

"I'm glad to tell you this is the greatest victory that I've ever had!"

"Why do you say that?"

"Don't you know who Jesus was? You notice I said 'was'! Ha! Ha! He was God getting into the act. Jesus came to battle us on man's terms and to recapture man from us. I don't mind telling you now that we have had a hard time the past thirty-three years."

"It seems that Jesus would have been at your mercy since he came as a man."

"It may seem that way, but he was different from other men. Everything we tried failed. When he was born, it took me so long to marshal my forces to kill him that he escaped. Every effort I made in the following years failed, too. But it was these last three years that we really had a battle."

"What was different about these three years?"

"Jesus went on the offensive. I thought I had him stopped at the beginning of his ministry when I tempted him in the wilderness, but he wouldn't break. Then I tried to expose him before his time by having my demons identify him as the Son of the most high God. Later I instigated an opposition front by using the religious leaders to bait him and to discredit him. Somehow he always slipped out of my trap. I even infiltrated his disciples. In fact, that is how I finally won. One of them betrayed him to the religious leaders. I knew I had him last night when he begged his

Father to let him out."

"So you were behind his capture?"

"Right. I had him killed. Just in time, too. He was leading a group of people to crown him king and set up a heavenly kingdom on earth."

"So you're satisfied that it's all over?"

"Of course. God's Son is dead. His disciples are in disarray. Jesus' ministry has been discredited. Most important, God is discredited."

"Won't God do something else?"

"No, that is the beautiful part. You see, God limited himself in the beginning to what man could do. Jesus represented mankind. But he died. God even turned away from him. Didn't you hear Jesus cry out just before he died, 'My God, my God, why hast thou forsaken me?' At the very last he admitted I had won when he said, 'It is finished.' If God's own Son could not defeat me, there is no hope for man. Tell the world: 'Satan has won; the war is over. I am now lord of the earth.' Excuse me, they want me back at the party. This is my inauguration."

If you did not know prophecy and Jesus' own predictions, it might appear that Satan had won the battle. But God's counteroffensive, the resurrection, gained the victory. Jesus did not succumb to death; he plundered it! He was not conquered by death; he conquered death.

The physical, bodily resurrection of Jesus firmly established God's invasion of history. The empty tomb and his appearances to the believers authenticated it. Jesus actually ate, was handled, and transformed believers. Jesus' resurrection body was more than his physical body. He walked through locked doors, disappeared, and appeared at will; but he was the same Jesus whom the disciples had seen, heard, and handled.

When Jesus emerged from the tomb, a new age broke on the world. Mankind had a new king. Jesus revealed through the resurrection that he had gained all authority in heaven and in earth (Matt. 28:18). He ruled over sin, death, and every created power. He had reconciled the world to God (2 Cor. 5:18-19; Col. 1:20).

Jesus' resurrection proved that the evil forces of Satan had been conquered throughout the cosmos. In his death and resurrection, Jesus "spoiled principalities and powers, he made a shew of them openly, triumphing over them" (Col. 2:15).

No longer is there any doubt who will win the conflict of the kingdoms. The decisive battle has been won over Satan. You might say that Satan continues to defeat Christians and to retard kingdom progress, but the outcome is no longer in doubt. Perhaps we could compare it to a decisive play in a ball game. The game may not be over, but it is obvious who the winner will be. D-day occurred in the battle between God and Satan when Jesus died and rose from the dead.

Man had rejected God's direct ruling over him in the Old Testament times, but God had worked through the covenant made at Sinai and through the covenant made with David to once again become Lord and King (Phil. 2:9-11; Eph. 1:20-21).

The greatest creative act of all time was the resurrection of Jesus. Its power is manifested most clearly in the new birth (2 Cor. 5:17). The resurrection revealed the nature of God. His love, power, presence, and purpose took on added meaning. Jesus shed his self-imposed limitations and revealed his eternal nature. The resurrection became the touchstone of the gospel. Prior to the resurrection the gospel was not preached to the nations because the good news had not all come to pass. The resurrection brought new meaning to the incarnation and death of Christ. Now the whole gospel could be preached and was preached by the first-century Christians, revealing that God had brought salvation to man in Jesus Christ.

When Paul tried to illustrate to the Ephesians how much power was available to them, he did not use a tornado, or an earthquake, or a volcano. Had the hydrogen bomb already been invented, he would not have used it as an example of power. All such illustrations of power are destructive. Paul illustrated creative power when he prayed that the Ephesians' eyes might be opened to know "what is the exceeding greatness of his power to us-ward who believe, according to the working of his mighty power, which he wrought in Christ, when he raised him from the dead" (Eph. 1:19-20).

As ruler of this age, God has "raised him from the dead, and set him at his own right hand in the heavenly places, far above all principality, and power, and might, and dominion, and every name that is named, not only in this world, but also in that which is to come" (Eph. 1:20-21).

Hallelujah! We live in the new age!

The resurrection ushered in the last days. We live between the resurrection and the return of Christ. During these times the gospel is to be preached to all nations. Jesus said, "This gospel of the kingdom shall be preached in all the world for a witness unto all nations; and then shall the end come" (Matt. 24:14).

The resurrection cut across all national and racial lines to present us with a universal, spiritual, omnipotent, and omnipresent Christ. Christ transcended his historical framework. People of all nations identify with him and claim him as their own. The resurrection forced Christianity to break with Judaism. Christ could not be contained by one race. The resurrection of Christ demands worldwide proclamation that "Jesus is Lord!"

Jesus gave the Great Commission on the basis of his resurrection. The resurrection was the condition for world missions. It made Jesus the supreme authority in the missionary enterprise. He had wrested the whole world, both visible and invisible, from the grip of all other powers. Therefore, God's people are sent forth in the triumphant name of the Lord Jesus Christ!

On five occasions after the resurrection, Jesus commanded his followers to be his witnesses. Each command was stated differently but embodied the same purpose.

PERSONAL LEARNING ACTIVITY 17
Read Matthew 28:18-20; Mark 16:15; Luke 24:46-49; John 20:21-23; and Acts 1:8. After reading these commands, summarize them in the form of a short, personal letter from Christ to you and your church.

We who have heard the gospel all our lives may not realize what good news it is. The incarnation tells the masses that God cares; the crucifixion proclaims forgiveness of sin; the resurrection shouts that the victory has been won over sin, death, and Satan.

Compare the good news of the gospel with the belief of my Buddhist friend in Indonesia whose greatest hope is to be absorbed into Nirvana, where his individual personality will no longer exist. Or compare it to my Hindu friend's hope for a better reincarnation next time, and the time after that, and so forth, until she can escape life, the evil "wheel of existence." Or compare it to my Moslem friend who hopes that God will forgive him and allow him into heaven but has no assurance. Or compare it to my animistic friend who long ago lost sight of the "high God" and is content to placate the spirits that inhabit the trees, the rocks, and the cemeteries. The gospel is God's good news. Deep in the heart of every man who hears it is a desire to believe it even when his religious traditions and sins bind him.

A sixty-five-year-old man heard about the Baptist church in the nearby village of Wonosekar, Java. His interests drew him to the service. He was amazed when the preacher read a holy book in his mother tongue, Javanese. He was astounded at the message of the gospel. Not long afterward, he embraced Christ as his Savior and said, "This is what I've been longing for and hoping for all my life."

The Christ-event divides history into two parts—B.C. and A.D. Too many people today live on the other side of Christ. They have never heard the gospel. For them it is still B.C.

BIBLIOGRAPHY

Conner, W. T. *The Cross in the New Testament*. Nashville: Broadman Press, 1944.
Fisher, Fred L. *Falling Walls: the Doctrine of Reconciliation*. Nashville: Convention Press, 1973.
Flew, Newton. *Jesus and His Church*. Nashville: Abingdon Press, 1938.
Forsyth, P. T. *The Work of Christ*. London: Independent Press, Ltd., 1938.
Kepler, Thomas. *The Meaning and Mystery of the Resurrection*. New York: Association Press, 1963.

CHAPTER 4

Mission of the Holy Spirit

"I want to give you something," said a ten-year-old boy as he slipped up to me after Vacation Bible School one day.
"Fine; what is it?"
"This," he said, shoving into my hand a small rock shaped like a heart. "I found it, and I want to give it to you."
"Thank you, but why do you want to give it to me?"
"Because I gave my heart to Jesus when you preached."

The coming of the Holy Spirit made possible the fulfillment of Ezekiel 36:26-27: "A new heart also will I give you, and a new spirit will I put within you: and I will take away the stony heart out of your flesh, and I will give you an heart of flesh. And I will put my spirit within you, and cause you to walk in my statutes."

The disciples must have felt like soldiers during a lull on the battlefield after they had lost their general. They did not know what to do, and they feared what the strangely quiet enemy might be doing. They hiked back to the upper room where Jesus had met them so many times, both before and after the resurrection. Their minds must have been flooded with questions such as: If we were not able to hold out while Jesus was with us, what can we do without him? How can we be witnesses to the hostile world that has just killed our Lord? What will the Holy Spirit do that Jesus has not done? How long should we wait? How will we know when the Holy Spirit comes? Why doesn't God do something quickly before some of our number run? In desperation, perhaps, they began to pray with one accord!

Meanwhile, Satan's review of his own situation could have been something like this. "Jesus has defeated me and has returned to heaven, but he has left his defenseless disciples as easy prey. As disorganized and as confused as they are, they will be vulnerable to a frontal attack. They have never understood that the war is being fought in the spiritual realm and, therefore, are still considering natural phenomena. I will have no trouble with them and need not even attack for a few days unless they try something."

Today we face the same basic problem the disciples faced—trying to fight spiritual battles with human resources. A majority of Christians live and serve as if Pentecost had never happened. They bravely try to obey Christ's commands in their own strength; yet they wonder how Satan so often outsmarts and overpowers them.

They ignore the mission of the Holy Spirit, who came to take Jesus' place, to inspire, to empower, and to guide them. For them, the Holy Spirit is almost the "unknown God," because they think of him as an influence, an attitude, or just another way to express the omnipresence of God.

The answer lies in the reality of experiencing the Holy Spirit's presence and power as the disciples did at Pentecost. Pentecost cannot be repeated anymore than Calvary can, but the power of Pentecost can be appropriated as surely as the redemption of Calvary can.

The lull between the ascension of Jesus and the coming of the Holy Spirit was not accidental. Little did Satan realize God's next step. Satan can read the Scriptures, and even misquote them for his own ends, but he cannot understand them because the Holy Spirit does not illuminate them for him. He rested for ten days, thinking the field had been vacated and the game forfeited, not knowing it was only halftime.

Why did the Holy Spirit delay his coming for ten days? Of course, it is impossible for us to be certain. There are several possibilities. First, it could have been a sacred moment in heaven. Jesus had returned from his successful mission on earth. The Holy Spirit was preparing to continue that mission. It must have been a great time of rejoicing and of anticipation. In retrospect, Peter said, "Therefore being by the right hand of God exalted, and having received of the Father the promise of the Holy Ghost, he [Jesus] hath shed forth this, which ye now see and hear" (Acts 2:33).

Meanwhile on earth, the second reason for the delay could have been the preparation needed by the disciples. As the followers of Jesus waited, they studied the Word in the light of the crucifixion and the resurrection. They rehearsed the past events and agreed on their doctrine. They agreed in prayer that they wanted the promise of the Father to come upon them. How it increased their anticipation and expectation!

The third reason for the delay was God's eternal plan. The Holy Spirit could not descend until the feast of Pentecost. God had planned for the Son to be crucified at the Feast of the Passover, because it symbolized Israel's redemption from Egypt and death through the sacrificial lamb. He had planned for the Holy Spirit to descend at Pentecost, because it symbolized the firstfruits of the harvest. The day the Harvester came, three thousand firstfruits were gathered into the kingdom.

Pentecost fully ushered in the "last days," the period between the coming of the Holy Spirit and the second coming of Christ. We live in those days. This is harvesttime. The Harvester has come to "reprove the world of sin, and of righteousness, and of judgment" (John 16:8) and to glorify Jesus (John 16:14). Since the advent of the Holy Spirit, God is intent on putting all things under the feet of Jesus as Lord and subduing all things. "Then cometh the end, when he shall have delivered up the kingdom to God, even the Father; when he shall have put down all rule and all authority and power. For he must reign, till he hath put all enemies under his feet" (1 Cor. 15:24-25).

PERSONAL LEARNING ACTIVITY 18
Write in your own words the three possible reasons for the ten-day delay between the ascension of Christ and the advent of the Holy Spirit.

THE INSPIRER OF MISSIONS

The mission of Christ could not be accomplished without the mission of the Holy Spirit. The Holy Spirit came to make God's people into the body of Christ. Christ had come to be with man; the Holy Spirit came to be in him. Through the Spirit, God enables man to become all he wants him to be. He is born of the Spirit and baptized into Christ's body at conversion (John 3:6-7; 1 Cor. 12:13). Prior to Christ's coming, the Holy Spirit came upon certain individuals for brief periods of time to accomplish specific tasks. After Pentecost, he came to live within each Christian forever and to minister through him in all events of life.

The Holy Spirit performs varied ministries within the body of Christ; he regenerates, sanctifies, teaches, guides, comforts, illuminates, and intercedes. But the most important ministry in relation to his mission is the filling of Christians for service. When Christians were filled with the Holy Spirit at Pentecost, they spontaneously shared the wonderful works of God with the people of many nations (Acts 2:4-11). The Spirit so inspired the first disciples that Peter had to explain what was happening. He said that the pouring out of the Spirit was the fulfillment of Joel's prophecy that "your sons and your daughters shall prophesy, and your young men shall see visions; and your old men shall dream dreams" (Acts 2:17). Moses' wish had come true: "Would God that all the Lord's people were prophets, and that the Lord would put his spirit upon them!" (Num. 11:29). The outpouring of the Holy Spirit inspired the overflowing witness of the saints. They were so inflamed that when they were scattered by persecution, they went everywhere telling the Word.

The Holy Spirit is the executor and the administrator of the Great Commission. He, rather than the Great Commission, is the motivator of missions. The Bible does not mention the Great Commission after Christ's ascension. Why? Perhaps the early church did not need it because the Holy Spirit had thrust them into missions and witness. If we were more sensitive to the Holy Spirit, we might not need to lean on obedience to the Great Commission as our primary motivation.

Since 1792, when William Carey urged Baptists to be missionaries to other lands, the Great Commission has been the basis of the modern missions movement. The Great Commission crystallizes Christ's command in one brief statement, but it is the Holy Spirit who inspires men to carry it out spontaneously. How different it is to share the message out of obligation and to share it out of spontaneous, overflowing love!

Harry Boer in his book *Pentecost and Missions* illustrates this difference in motivation by the story of Adam and Eve. God commanded Adam and Eve to be fruitful and replenish the earth (Gen. 1:28). However, they responded, not in obedience to a command, but because God had placed in them a desire to consummate their marriage and have children. Just so, when the Holy Spirit fills the Christian, he places a desire in the heart to fulfill the Commission.

If we are to experience a massive missions movement in our day, it will have to be motivated by the power of the Holy Spirit filling the people of God. When God's people are revived, they witness. Any "revival" that does not result in Christians witnessing and in sinners coming to Christ has not been an outpouring of the Holy Spirit.

PERSONAL LEARNING ACTIVITY 19
Examine your witness and that of your church to see if "this is that" which was prophesied by Joel and experienced by the disciples at Pentecost (Acts 2:16-18). List the similarities and the differences.

THE EMPOWERER OF THE CHURCH

The disciples asked Jesus just before he ascended if the kingdom would be restored to Israel at that time (Acts 1:7). He told them that the Father kept the timetable and they were not to be concerned about the kind of power (*ekousia*) that comes from having authority. He said, on the other hand, that they were to be concerned about the kind of power the Holy Spirit brought to make them worldwide witnesses. Here Jesus used the word *dunamis*, from which we get the words *dynamo* and *dynamite*.

The power they received with the filling of the Holy Spirit was life-changing and world-changing because it was living, spiritual power.

The lordship of Christ gives the believer *authority* to bear witness to everyone. The presence of the Holy Spirit gives him the spiritual *ability* to make an impact on those hearing the testimony. The Spirit-filled believer never witnesses alone. The Holy Spirit works within the lost person to verify and to personalize the witness of the believer. He makes real the authority and the presence of Christ.

To witness without the power of the Holy Spirit is folly. Only the Holy Spirit can convict of sin, judgment, and righteousness (John 16:8-11). God's mission demands God's power. The power of the Holy Spirit is available to every believer who allows him to invade fully his life.

The filling of the Spirit is not a nebulous experience which you can only hope to possess. It is a definite, recognizable experience. Every believer has the Spirit within him from the time he experiences the new birth (Rom. 8:16-17). However, all believers are not continually filled with the power of the Spirit. Jesus commanded his disciples not to leave Jerusalem until the Holy Spirit came upon them. Look at Peter to see the difference before and after the filling of the Spirit (compare Luke 22:54-62 with Acts 4:5-12). See the boldness of the disciples when they were refilled with the Spirit (Acts 4:31). Note that the Ephesians were filled after they had been saved and baptized in Jesus' name (Acts 19:5-6).

Yes, the filling of the Spirit is a definite experience to equip God's people for service. Ideally, it should occur initially when one is converted, as it did in the case of Cornelius (Acts 10:44-45). Tragically, most Christians go years without knowing the difference between being indwelled by the Spirit and being filled with the Spirit.

The Bible commands all believers to be filled with the Spirit. "Be not drunk with wine, wherein is excess; but be filled with the Spirit" (Eph. 5:18). Most Christians are more adamant about the negative command not to be drunk with wine than they are about the positive one to be filled with the Spirit. The Greek verb in Ephesians 5:18 makes it clear that being filled is a continual, repeated action. Every Christian is indwelled by the Holy Spirit from the moment of his conversion (John 3:5-6; Rom. 8:16), but every Christian needs to be filled continually with the Spirit. The filling of the Spirit gave the disciples boldness, wisdom, and the ability to witness. This scared, frightened, cowering group of defeated disciples experienced what it meant to be a part of the living body of Christ ministering to the world.

While I was a freshman in college, the Holy Spirit created in my heart an overwhelming desire to bear witness to Christ. In the months that followed, his presence overcame my natural shyness and thrust me out several times each week onto the streets and into bars to witness. However, I was not successful in leading people to Christ. I memorized Scriptures, studied soul-winning books, and prayed. But something was missing.

One day I received in the mail a booklet that told of the experiences of D. L. Moody, R. A. Torrey, Billy Sunday, Billy Graham, and others whose ministries had been transformed when they experienced the filling of the Holy Spirit.

I had a burning desire to be used of God, but I could not find anyone who could tell me how to be filled. Finally, a friend loaned me the book *The Holy Spirit: Who He Is and What He Does* by R. A. Torrey.

For the first time, I realized that the Holy Spirit is a person who possesses us, instead of a power or an influence that we possess. Torrey showed that the Holy Spirit, who lives within us, wants to fill us for service. By the next evening I had finished the book and was ready to follow its instructions on being filled with the Spirit. I confessed all my sins, presented myself fully to God, and asked in faith for the Holy Spirit to fill me. As I confessed my sins, I realized how much the Holy Spirit had loved me and had been grieved by my ignoring him. Then I presented my body, will, emotions, intellect, and spirit to be used by God in any way. The most difficult part was accepting by faith the filling of the Holy Spirit without any outward sign or manifestation. I told God, "I will accept the fact that I am filled with the Spirit on the basis of faith in the Word, no matter what happens when I witness." There was no great emotional experience, but I had a deep awareness of the love of the Spirit.

The next morning when I went to class, the grass looked greener and the birds sang more sweetly. I was so aware of the Spirit's presence that I wanted to move over on the sidewalk to let him walk beside me. That evening I witnessed to a boy on the street, and he accepted Christ as his Savior. Two nights later two black teenagers accepted Christ. The following night a man professed faith in Christ, the night after that another man.

I remarked to a friend: "I don't see how this can continue. Every night I go out to witness, someone accepts Christ." That night no one did. I had to come back and ask forgiveness and be filled afresh because I had dared to think that I had won those people to Christ myself. God willingly refilled me with his Spirit when I was willing to confess my sins, present myself, and ask in faith. Once again people began to come to Christ.

In the twenty-five years since that experience, the Holy Spirit has taught me the secret of being filled for each task of service. Thousands of times I have had to ask him to refill me when I have sinned, and he has done so. The filling of the Spirit energizes and empowers different gifts in different persons, but in every case the result brings glory to Christ and attracts others to him. In chapter 8 we will examine more carefully the gifts of the Spirit.

PERSONAL LEARNING ACTIVITY 20
Read Psalm 139:23-24. Ask the Lord to point out any sins that would prevent his filling you with the Holy Spirit. Confess those sins to him. Present yourself to him (Rom. 12:1-2) and ask him to fill you (Luke 11:13; 1 John 5:14-15).

THE GUIDE IN MISSIONS
As executor of Christ's will, the Holy Spirit determines the course of missions. Twelve times in the book of Acts it appears the witness might have been confined and that the disciples

might have been satisfied with gains already made. But each time the Holy Spirit thrust them farther into the fields. Acts 1:8 outlines the Spirit's movement: Jerusalem (Acts 2:1 to 8:4); Judea and Samaria (Acts 8:5 to 12:25); and the remainder of the world (Acts 13:1 to 28:31).

When persecution came, the disciples prayed, and "they were all filled with the Holy Ghost, and they spake the word of God with boldness" (Acts 4:31). Later the persecution became an instrument of the Spirit so that "they that were scattered abroad went every where preaching the word" (Acts 8:4).

Philip went to the outcast Samaritans. Strangely enough, in the midst of a great spiritual ingathering in Samaria, the Spirit told Philip to go to the desert and to witness to one man. How often the guidance of the Spirit conflicts with the wisdom of man! Nevertheless, Philip obediently followed the Spirit's guidance and won an important Ethiopian official who took the gospel back to his native land (Acts 8:26-40).

It appeared that the witness might be confined to the Jews and Jewish proselytes until the Spirit got Peter's attention with a vision and sent him to witness to Cornelius (Acts 10). The Spirit had more difficulty getting Peter ready to go than he had with Cornelius who was eagerly waiting to hear. How often this is the case because we fail to follow the guidance of the Holy Spirit.

Another breakthrough occurred when Greeks in Antioch were saved. One year later the Holy Spirit separated Barnabas and Paul from the Antioch church to send them a step farther into the world with the gospel.

When Paul and his friends returned with the good news that the Gentiles had turned to God, it seemed that the Jewish element in the Jerusalem church might shackle the witness by demanding that Gentiles first become Jews. Once again the Holy Spirit intervened, and they wrote, "It seemed good to the Holy Ghost, and to us, to lay upon you no greater burden than these necessary things" (Acts 15:28).

Paul and his co-laborers experienced the direct guidance of the Spirit to go to Philippi, but it came one step at a time. First, the Holy Spirit had to forbid them to speak the word in Asia (Acts 16:6). Then he did not allow them to go to Bithynia (Acts 16:7). Since he had been forbidden to go left or right, Paul assumed he should go straight ahead. But when he reached the Mediterranean Sea at Troas, he had received no further instructions. That night Paul had a vision of a man from Macedonia saying, "Come over into Macedonia, and help us" (Acts 16:9), and they deduced that God must be leading them in that direction (Acts 16:10).

Only the Spirit is qualified to determine the place of service for his people. We are so limited in our understanding that we cannot predict the next move of the Spirit.

Paul could not have understood all the experiences the Spirit took him through to lead him to Rome, but who questions that it was God's will? Surely more than once the situation appeared foolish to Paul, but he never lost sight of his mission to the Gentiles and of his faith in the leadership of the Spirit (Acts 26:16-18).

God reveals our mission to the nations through the Bible, but the time and place for carrying it out is to be revealed by the Holy Spirit as he chooses. One fact is certain—Christians are to witness wherever the Holy Spirit has placed them until he directs them to another place. If a Christian is not being a missionary where he is, he need not expect to be led somewhere else to be a missionary. The Holy Spirit usually guides his people nearby before sending them on a distant mission.

Do not misunderstand. The Holy Spirit does not classify missions in one locale as better than in another locale. Anyone who thinks foreign missions is better than home missions has failed to realize that the Holy Spirit has charge of world missions. A person saved in one country is no more or no less valuable than one saved in another country.

Nevertheless, the Holy Spirit redistributes the harvesters from an area where there are many laborers to other places where there are few laborers. He must determine the need and redeploy the forces. When out of each five thousand Southern Baptists only one is a home missionary and one a foreign missionary, we have to wonder if we are allowing the Holy Spirit to select, to separate, and to send forth laborers into the harvest as he wants. We are all the people of God. Perhaps we are not spending enough time in fasting and in prayer to listen to the Spirit's guidance as the Christians at Antioch did (Acts 13:2-3).

PERSONAL LEARNING ACTIVITY 21
List three ways the Holy Spirit fulfills his mission.

The Holy Spirit periodically breaks through the traditions and the prejudices of his people to thrust them out into the world as flaming witnesses. His moving among the Indonesian Baptist missionaries of Central Java in 1971 spread to missionaries throughout the country and several other Southeast Asia countries. He changed lives and structures so radically that a new mission strategy for reaching the lost was named "The New Pattern."

The spiritual awakening began with brokenness over sin. On the first night of a prayer retreat, an atmosphere of acceptance was created that freed us to be honest. One person broke down and confessed his sins. Revival began as always with one person's being honest with God and with his fellowmen. For two hours, the twenty-five missionaries confessed their barrenness, their emptiness, and their powerlessness. A spirit of expectancy rose the next day as various ones shared their experiences of being filled with the Spirit. Others shared insights from the book *The Shantung Revival*. The Spirit probed deeply into motives, relationships, and actions. Hypocrisy, bitterness, lust, hate, gumblings, skepticism, selfishness, covetousness, and other sins of the flesh and the spirit were laid at the Lord's feet. Lives were committed afresh to Christ, and the Spirit's filling was claimed by faith. The planned program was laid aside as the Spirit took control. Mealtimes and bedtimes were postponed or ignored.

The men's group was engrossed in urgent prayers for the lost and the sick. Some sobbed uncontrollably. Others fell face down on the floor. All worshiped the holy God. Someone began singing "The Lord's Prayer" and, as others joined in, it was as if the Great Conductor led in the most beautiful rendition of the song any had ever heard.

Each day the awesome presence of God was felt. The worship times did not follow usual patterns, but nothing offensive intruded. Testimonies of victory moved into songs of thanksgiving and praise and prayers of intercession. When the weekend retreat ended at 2:00 A.M. Monday, all knew that the Holy Spirit had moved among us to prepare us for some special ministry. One China veteran said: "When God sends revival, it is to prepare his people for harvest or for persecution. In China, it was for persecution. I don't know what he is preparing us for, but he has gotten us ready."

Missionaries from other areas began to ask what had happened to change our lives so dramatically, only to be convicted themselves and later filled with the Spirit. Missionaries returned to their churches to confess to national Christians their bad attitudes. In many churches great numbers of people professed Christ, rededicated their lives, or committed themselves to service.

Four months later our prayers were answered as the Spirit moved among all the missionaries and their children at the annual meeting. Lives were changed radically. One mother who said that her Christian life had been like a Girl Scout fire, flaming up again and again only to go out, testifies to this day that the fire lit during the mission meeting is still burning. A missionary wife who confessed she had not seen a single person come to Christ as a direct result of her personal witness in fifteen years returned home to lead several to Christ.

The revival spilled over to the teenagers. Led by a Baptist Student Union summer missionary, they passed out five thousand tracts, conducted a street service, and moved the service into the home of a woman that they had led to Christ. The summer missionary's zeal knew no bounds. Throughout the rest of the summer, he daily rode his bicycle into the villages and rice fields, handing out tracts. Even though he did not know the language, he did more evangelism than many who did know the language.

A three-day strategy conference on mission work preceding the mission meeting extended to a full ten days of spiritual revival and resolute decision making that changed the structure of Baptist work in Indonesia and began to prepare God's people to reach 125 million Indonesians for Christ. The impact of the awakening and the changes coming out of it have been felt throughout Southeast Asia and other countries.

The Holy Spirit works throughout the world to prepare men's hearts for the gospel, but his primary work among God's people is to send them forth with the gospel message. To march into the battle without the guidance of the Spirit is as foolish as an army's marching into battle without a general. For us to testify of God's grace without the power of the Holy Spirit is to fight without weapons. Satan, the evil spirit, fights for control over the lives of those whom he has seduced. His grip can be broken only by the power of the Holy Spirit. The Spirit works through God's people to accomplish his mission.

BIBLIOGRAPHY
Allen, Roland. *The Ministry of the Spirit.* World Dominion Press, 1965.
————. *The Spontaneous Expansion of the Church.* Grand Rapids: William B. Eerdmans Publishing Company, 1962.
Boer, Harry R. *Pentecost and Missions.* Grand Rapids: William B. Eerdmans Publishing Company, 1961.

CHAPTER 5

Co-mission of the Church

*He was a handsome young man. His stylish
brown hair lay barely ruffled on the pillow. His
voice resonated like a bell in the small room as his
penetrating eyes captured me. A dimple danced
on the edge of his smile, and each movement of
his eyebrows revealed unexpressed feelings.
The only thing that marred this superb
specimen of a man was that he could hardly move
a muscle below his neck. His left arm jerked
spasmodically when he held small items. A
mysterious virus had immobilized him. I thought,
He is a parable of the modern church.*

The church lives with two identities. First, it is the remnant that
God has chosen, sanctified, and commissioned to be a blessing
to the world. Second, it is the body of Christ that must fulfill his
ministry in the world. It lives in tension between two realities—
the possibility of failing to accomplish God's purpose just as
Israel did and the possibility of becoming the fullness of Christ
(Eph. 1:22-23). Since Christ fulfilled all the Father's hopes for
Israel, the church as his body is to fulfill the same ministry to the
world.

THE CHURCH'S POSSIBILITIES AND GOD'S EXPECTATIONS

"The church is something like Noah's ark," said a late medieval
manuscript. "If it weren't for the storm outside, you couldn't
stand the smell inside."[1] Out of the deadness of the churches in
Europe and in America the cry has come, "God is dead!" Robert
Adolfs in his book *The Grave of God* said that if God is dead,
then the church is his grave. Men saw a dead church and
thought its owner was dead. The church has been maligned,

ridiculed, and given up for dead by many because it has not functioned as Christ's living body. The church is not dead, but to a cynical world it appears to be.

Jesus linked the people of God in the Old Testament with his new people in the New Testament. His choosing of twelve disciples symbolized the link with the twelve tribes of Israel. The disciples also symbolized the remnant that inherited Israel's promises. Jesus taught that the new remnant was spiritual rather than national. The church consists of the spiritual sons of Abraham.

In these last days since Pentecost, God has revealed the mystery of his church—to make of Jew and Gentiles a new creation. "That the Gentiles should be fellows-heirs, and of the same body and partakers of his promise in Christ by the gospel" (Eph. 3:6).

Since we have received the promises of God and in us all the families of the earth shall be blessed, we also must accept the responsibilities. To deny or to neglect these responsibilities puts us in the same position as Israel when she refused to be a nation of holy, servant-priests to the world. God judges unfaithful partners.

PERSONAL LEARNING ACTIVITY 22
Read Ephesians 1 and write in twenty-five words or less God's hope for his church.

Paul prayed that Christians would have their eyes opened so that they "may know what is the hope of his calling, and what the riches of the glory of his inheritance in the saints [is]" (Eph. 1:18). "His inheritance" mentioned in verse 18 is not our inheritance, but God's. God's amazing hope is that he will inherit something in us. God cannot inherit anything in this universe because it is already his. His inheritance is his people accomplishing his will. In the Old Testament the word *inheritance* is often called a *portion*. Deuteronomy 32:9 says, "For the Lord's portion is his people; Jacob is the lot of his inheritance." God's inheritance is the fruit of his work—that is, a holy people who do his will. Parents who have seen their fondest dreams fulfilled in their children should be able to understand how God can call his children his inheritance. He is made richer by the praises we give him and by the praises we cause others to give him because of our lives (Eph. 1:12). God expects us to be Christ's body, "the fulness of him that filleth all in all" (Eph. 1:23).

Although some may have given up hope for the church, God has not. For "Christ also loved the church, and gave himself for it; that he might sanctify and cleanse it with the washing of water by the word, that he might present it to himself a glorious church, not having spot, or wrinkle, or any such thing; but that it should be holy and without blemish" (Eph. 5:25-27).

PRIESTS OF GOD: THE CALVARY PRINCIPLE

As God's chosen generation, we live in the election stream of God's great purpose. This part of the chapter explores what it means to be chosen to be priests. Before reading on, complete the following personal learning activity.

PERSONAL LEARNING ACTIVITY 23
Compare Exodus 19:5-6 with 1 Peter 2:9-10 and list the similarities.

Formerly we were Christless, homeless, promiseless, hopeless, and Godless (Eph. 2:12). Just as the veil in the Temple barred man from the holy of holies, so our sins had created a barrier that kept us separated from God and each other. But now we have been made one with him and with each other by the blood of Christ. Jesus, as High Priest, opened the way to God for us. By his death he split the veil to the holy of holies, established a new covenant with us, and gave us direct access to God (Heb. 8:6-13). Christ redeemed us by his own sacrifice and gave us even greater promises than Israel received (2 Pet. 1:3-4).

As the royal priesthood, we receive both the promises and the responsibilities of the new covenant. As royalty, we live in the blessedness of the kingdom; as priests, we function as kingdom representatives.

All of us are New Testament priests and have specific duties differing from the duties of the priests in the Old Testament. The Old Testament priests sacrificed animals; New Testament priests sacrifice their living bodies, praise, thanksgiving, good works, and material possessions (Rom. 12:1; Heb. 13:15). Old Testament priests obeyed and ministered only the Torah; we obey and minister the entire Word. Old Testament priests ministered in the Temple at Jerusalem; we are the temple of the Holy Spirit (1 Cor. 3:16) and minister all over the world. Old Testament priests, as representatives of God, pronounced blessings on individual people; we bless all nations by who we are and what we do. The Old Testament priesthood was limited to the tribe of Levi; the New Testament priesthood includes all believers.

Christ, the High Priest, offered the supreme sacrifice in the crucifixion. We are commanded to deny ourselves, take up our crosses daily, and follow Christ (Luke 9:23).

PERSONAL LEARNING ACTIVITY 25
List at least three reasons why you think all believers should function as priests in the world.

All God's children should function as priests to the world because God elected them. He individually chose each Christian to be a part of his people to bless all the families of the earth. Jesus sacrificed himself for the sins of the world and gave to his people the ministry of reconciliation. The Holy Spirit indwells every believer and places him in his holy, spiritual temple designated to bless all nations. The Great Commission outlines the task of every believer as a priest to the world. Every Christian priest makes up the body of Christ which functions as Christ in the world. If we recapture the priesthood of the believers, we will assure a witness to all men.

As a holy nation, we are a peculiar people and should live separated lives. We should be different in our thoughts, talk, and walk. The world searches for a people who offer something different from what they have known. Our lives should be to the praise of God's glory so that when people come in contact with us, they will praise him. We were chosen "that we should be holy and without blame before him . . . to the praise of the glory of his grace . . . that we should be to the praise of his glory, who first trusted in Christ" (Eph. 1:4-12).

We are chosen, made priests, and become a holy nation for one reason—that we should show forth the praises of him who called us out of darkness into his marvelous light (1 Pet. 2:9). We, as God's go-between with the world, bear witness to his grace in saving power. As each believer has the privilege and the responsibility to go to the Father to obtain forgiveness, so every believer has the privilege and the responsibility to go to the world to tell men of God's forgiveness. It is almost unthinkable that we who have been forgiven such a huge debt would not be eager to share the good news that forgiveness is available to everyone. To fail to go to the nations short-circuits God's purpose in making us his people.

SERVANTS OF GOD: THE INCARNATION PRINCIPLE
The church, as the body of Christ, is incarnate in the world to become the Suffering Servant. It is not called out of the world but called to go into the world and love like Christ, forgive like Christ, and give itself to the world like Christ.

PERSONAL LEARNING ACTIVITY 26
Read John 20:21; 15:20; and Philippians 1:29. Compare Jesus' role as a servant with our own.

For Jesus, incarnation meant emptying himself, becoming obedient, and dying. Some missionaries have followed literally

Christ's example and become martyrs. But a more common application of the incarnation principle is to empty ourselves of earthly power and self-importance. Robert Adolfs says:

> If the Church is to have a future, she must renounce all claims to power and all longing for power, all honour, worldly esteem and love of display. For Christ's sake, she will have to become "poor" in the deepest evangelical sense of the word. In order to win everything, she will have to be ready to lose everything. She will have to be a *Servant*—a Servant who will not use power to force men to action, but who will aim to rule only by love.
>
> A kenotic [self-emptying] Church will also make the spread of the gospel on a world-wide scale possible for the first time. The Church in the form of service will no longer be bound to Western forms of Christianity and will be able to be present, as a servant . . . .[2]

The incarnational nature of the church runs counter to the modern mind-set. Even missionaries often are esteemed for their education, skill, and affluence in underprivileged societies. In assuming the leadership role, they sometimes subconsciously make servants of the nationals. How different was Jesus' entrance to this world. He emptied himself and became a servant. The attitude of the servant has not permeated the mentality of many servants of God, even in our own country. The pastor is treated as one to be served more often than as a servant. To be effective missionaries to the world, Americans must learn the servant role that Jesus took.

Jesus made the servant role explicit to his disciples in Matthew 23, a passage many of us skip because we do not consider ourselves hypocrites. He condemned the self-serving Pharisees and warned his followers not to be like them. He told his disciples that they should not allow people to call them rabbi, father, or master. Each of these titles shows an attitude of superiority instead of a servant heart. A teacher (rabbi) assumes superiority because of his knowledge. A father assumes a superior position of authority because of his age, experience, or relationship. A master (leader) expects others to serve him because he has been given authority on the basis of charisma, possessions, or delegation. Jesus said we should not let others use any of these designations for us, because we have only one Father who is in heaven and only one Master who is Christ.

Jesus said, "But he that is greatest among you shall be your servant" (Matt. 23:11). He meant for us to be permanent servants. Many times we think servanthood is only the way to becoming a master eventually. But the exaltation Christ promised occurs in heaven rather than on earth. Servanthood is not simply a temporary debasing of oneself in order to become a master. Jesus' example shows us that we should be serving the poor and needy of the world, whether they be in an urban ghetto or in a foreign country.

PERSONAL LEARNING ACTIVITY 27
Write a paragraph explaining in your own words what it means for the church to be incarnate in the world.

Late one night I heard a timid knock on the door of our home in Bogor, Indonesia. As I opened the door, a woman, obviously upset, said: "Sir, I live down in the village. My baby has a high fever. We can't get it down. We need some ice cubes. We have no refrigerator. Can you help me?" A few moments later as she hurried out with a bulging bag of ice cubes, she gave me the greatest compliment I have ever received. She said: "Thank you so much. I had not met you before tonight, and I was scared to knock on your door. But I knew you are a *hamba Tuhan* (servant of God). So I thought you would be glad to help me."

Whoever gives a cup of cold water in Jesus' name, even if it is frozen into cubes, will not lose his reward. One factor that amazes the world perhaps more than any other is the church's myriad of service ministries to those who cannot help themselves. The church or the Christian that identifies with Christ will serve him by serving men.

The purpose of service focuses on the proclamation of the gospel. Proclamation grows most naturally out of a life of service. Because one serves he has opportunity to testify. Jesus' order was first to do and then to teach (Acts 1:1). Living the servant-life evokes close examination by the world and provides the right occasion—surely the best occasion—for witness.

Christ's crucifixion best illustrates our role as priests. His incarnation best illustrates the servant attitude. His resurrection best illustrates our role as sons of the King.

SONS OF THE KING: THE RESURRECTION PRINCIPLE

From the time God created the world, his intention was to rule over obedient persons. The Bible often refers to Israel's wandering in the wilderness and entering of the Promised Land as the prototype period, because God led them directly. After they rebelled and asked for a king, God began a new process that would ultimately result in his direct rule over them through King Jesus, of the line of David. As King over all, Jesus seeks men to crown him Lord of their lives. He offers sonship to all who accept his lordship.

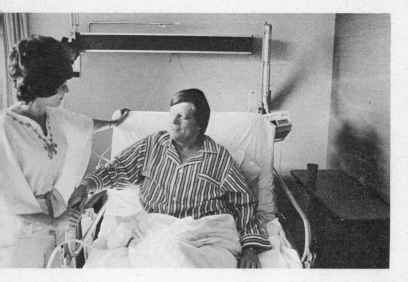

As God's children we have an intimate relationship and an inherited interest in the kingdom. Jesus shared his heart with children of the kingdom to involve them in establishing it. He said, "It is your Father's good pleasure to give you the kingdom" (Luke 12:32).

As children of the King, we announce that the kingdom has come. With joy we tell the good news that our Father owns everything. The new age has come, and as his children we inherit what our Father rightly owns. If we do not proclaim God's kingdom, who will? Satan is most effective in defeating the kingdom of God when he prevents God's children from witnessing.

The first church faced almost insurmountable odds. Satan unleashed his attacks in ever increasing force and cunning, but the early Christians would not be silent. The book of Acts depicts four strategies Satan used to prevent the church from fulfilling its co-mission. No matter what devices Satan may use to tempt man, man is always responsible for his actions. The early church depended on the Holy Spirit for victory. The church today faces the same problems.

First, Satan used the enemies of God to persecute the church of God. The early Christians were threatened, beaten, and some were killed; but they would not be silent. When the Jewish leaders threatened, they continued to speak out and even prayed for more boldness (Acts 4:20,29). When they were beaten, they praised God for counting them worthy to suffer shame for him (Acts 5:41). As they were being killed, they prayed that their enemies be forgiven (Acts 7:60). They said, "We are his witnesses of these things; and so is also the Holy Ghost" (Acts 5:32). Their witness resulted in thousands following Christ.

Second, Satan tried the more subtle tactic of seeking to divert the church from within. When Satan works within the church, he is more difficult to overcome. Ananias and Sapphira lied about their giving of their possessions for the needs of the body. God intervened directly lest the problem of selfishness, lying, and deception cut the taproot of love. After this, great fear fell on all people, "and believers were the more added to the Lord, multitudes both of men and women" (Acts 5:14).

Third, Satan moved even more deeply into the fellowship of the church to divide its loyalties. When the Greek widows began grumbling about injustice in the distribution of food to the Hebrew widows, the situation grew serious. These were honest people who perhaps had a legitimate gripe. If Satan could sow discord through prejudice, pity, and misplaced priorities, he could siphon off the church's enthusiasm for witnessing. Again the church sought God's leadership, and he led them to choose honest men, full of the Holy Spirit, wisdom, and faith to take care of this business. The result was that "the word of God increased; and the number of the disciples multiplied" (Acts 6:7).

Fourth, Satan mounted his gravest attack in the area of false doctrine. If doctrine is false, the church is false and the mission is lost. A leader for the church accused Peter of fellowshipping and eating with Gentiles. Later the council of elders entertained charges against Paul and Barnabas for preaching to the Gentiles. Both instances highlighted the problems of prejudice and the obstacles that had been raised to the universal application of the gospel. Once again they prayed, and the Holy Spirit led them to accept anyone who would believe the gospel. The result was missions to the Gentiles and opening of the doors of the kingdom to all people, including us.

PERSONAL LEARNING ACTIVITY 28
List one modern instance to illustrate each of these obstacles that cause the church not to fulfill its co-mission with God.

1. Persecution _____

2. Deception _____

3. Discord _____

4. Prejudice _____

In 1972 I was allowed to witness a denomination begin to become God's missionary people. I was invited to preach at the *Kerapatan Gereja Protestant Indonesia*, a convention of churches in North Minahasa, Indonesia, with Baptist beliefs. Their leaders had been graduated from the Indonesian Baptist Theological Seminary, and many of them had pastored Baptist churches earlier in Java. At their triennial convention I spoke on "God's Plan for World Redemption Through the Spiritual Ministry of All His People."

Each day began with prayer at 5:00 A.M. The first morning several came two and one-half hours early! I was awakened by their singing at 4:00 A.M. Conversational prayer was introduced to them, and God used it to spark revival as they confessed their sins to God and to one another. Throughout the next day pastors stood in the convention meeting to confess such sins as spiritual apathy and hatred of each other. The third day when I taught about the Holy Spirit's ministry and filling, I asked those who wanted to be filled with the Spirit to kneel. I expected a few to do so. To my surprise, almost everyone knelt. Great soul-wrenching prayers went up to God as confessions were made to him, followed by praise for the refreshing showers of blessing. The awesome presence of the Spirit filled the place for the next hour as his servants poured out their hearts to him. During the week several pastors were saved.

They had given me several hours a day to expound the Scriptures on the themes you are studying in this book. In the final service I called for the dedication of the entire denomination to missionary service. From the beginning of the invitation the front was crowded with people who wanted to surrender themselves as missionaries, to give of their means to support missions, and to rededicate their lives to his service. The president of the convention called for pastors who already had made decisions to help others who were coming. So many made decisions that even then there were not enough to deal individually with each one. So he said: "This week we have learned that we're all priests. There are not enough pastors to help all of you, so minister to one another!" Never have I seen

God turn the leadership of a denomination so thoroughly upside down—or right side up! The president of the convention said: "This has been like an atomic bomb dropped on us. God has done this, and we will start to rebuild along his teachings." They immediately established a department of missions and began planning to send missionaries to other islands.

Two years later when I returned to preach in a missions conference, a large number of the finest pastors surrendered to go as missionaries to other islands. They said: "We must send our best men as missionaries. God will raise up other men to pastor the churches here at home. We will begin to train them now, using the extension seminary Baptists have pioneered in Java."

Today they have missionaries in Kalimantan (Borneo), Sumatra, Central Sulawesi, and several other islands. The son of one of their wealthiest families is in the jungles of Kalimantan leading several of their missionaries and establishing a seminary for Dayaks. They are embodying the mission of Christ as priests, servants, and sons of the King.

NOTES
1. Robert McAfee Brown, *The Significance of the Church* (Philadelphia: The Westminster Press, 1956), p. 17.
2. Robert Adolfs, *The Grave of God,* tr. N. D. Smith (New York: Harper & Row, Publishers, Inc., 1967), pp. 115, 148. Used by permission.

BIBLIOGRAPHY
Brown, Robert McAfee. *The Significance of the Church*. Philadelphia: The Westminster Press, 1956.
Criswell, W. A. *The Doctrine of the Church*. Nashville: Convention Press, 1980. (Available December 1980)
DeDietrich, Suzanne. *The Witnessing Community*. Philadelphia: The Westminster Press, 1958.
Heunel, Albert. *The Humiliation of the Church*. Philadelphia: The Westminster Press, 1966.
Hillman, Eugene. *The Church as Mission*. New York: Herder and Herder, 1965.
Margull, Hans. *Hope in Action: the Church's Task in the World*. Philadelphia: Muhlenburg Press, 1959.
Marty, Martin. *The Improper Opinion*. Philadelphia: The Westminster Press, 1961.

CHAPTER 6

Discipling: Mandate to Mission

Anyone can see the number of apples on a tree; only a few can see the number of trees in an apple.

Waves from the Malaka Strait splashed below me on the rocky shores of Penang, a small island off the west coast of the Malay Peninsula. A fisherman guided his boat into the bay and began his day's work. As is my custom, I asked God what he wanted to teach me from that situation.

He seemed to say: "What if you were given the task of catching every fish in the seven seas? How would you do it?" I was overwhelmed at the thought. Impossible! "But that is the job I have given you," he responded.

"There is no way," I said.

"What if," he broke into my thoughts, "every time the fisherman caught a fish and touched it, it changed into a man? The fisherman could then explain to the first fish-turned-man what had happened to him. He could tell him about the plight of his kinfish trapped in their watery prison and how they, too, can be freed by the touch of a human hand. He could teach the man to catch fish and to repeat the process. Soon their number would multiply."

"If we were doing it like most Christian training," I rejoined, "we would send the man who had been a fish to an institute of fisheries in the mountains. There he could learn about currents, sea life, oceanography, and so on. After three or four years he could return to help the first fisherman. Of course, he might not know how to throw a net or bait a hook."

"A much more practical way," the Lord whispered, "would be to show him immediately how to fish, thus letting him experience the joy of releasing another man from the fish condition. Then he could pass on what he had learned to the other new man. Someday he might need advanced study to help him teach others, but the immediate need would be to give him on-the-job training. If you would use this method, as I did, you could tell all the men in the world about me."

Jesus painstakingly discipled his followers for three years because he knew that the implementation of God's plan was to be in their hands. Yet by the end of his earthly ministry, all that remained were eleven original disciples, one hundred twenty other followers who attended the prayer vigil in the upper room, and five hundred who witnessed his ascension.

How few they must have seemed when Jesus commanded them to make disciples of all nations! Plainly, they needed to multiply. But Jesus had prepared them well for the coming rapid expansion recorded in the book of Acts.

THE IMPOSSIBLE TASK

Southern Baptists have committed themselves to taking the gospel to every person in the world by the year 2000. The population explosion makes such a task as impossible as it must have seemed when Jesus commissioned the first disciples.

World population has outstripped our comprehension. If we could have begun winning converts at the rate of one a minute the day Jesus arose, we would have won only one billion persons from then until now. Obviously, that is not fast enough to reach our world.

Suppose we could win three thousand persons a day as the disciples did at Pentecost. How long do you suppose it would take to win the approximately six billion persons expected to be on the earth in the year 2000? Fifty-four hundred seventy-nine years! If Abraham had won three thousand converts each day, and his descendants had continued doing so, it would be approximately A.D. 3000 before we could evangelize just the people who will be living on the earth in the year 2000.

In spite of the statistics, Baptists are saying we will share the gospel with everyone on earth by the year 2000. That means we have to witness to about 300 million different persons each year between 1980 and 2000. And that doesn't even count all those who die during those years. Our foreign missionary force will continue to operate at the ratio of one missionary to each 1.5 million people, even if the accelerated appointment pace doubles the number of missionaries by that time. All the modern means known to man cannot present effectively the message to that number of people each year, scattered as they are throughout the remote regions of the world.

Jesus did not flinch when he gave the command to preach the gospel to every creature. He had a plan; we must recover it. One part of that plan was to select a few men and pour his life into them. He discipled them and taught them by example to disciple others. His plan was followed by the first-century Christians until they had spread across the known world. Stated simply, the plan is this: one person is to disciple one or more until the one being discipled can disciple yet a third person. Then the two should win two others and disciple them, and so forth.

PERSONAL LEARNING ACTIVITY 29
To see how fast disciples can grow by multiplication, multiply 2 x 2. Continue to multiply the results each time by 2 for 33 times. Most pocket calculators have a constant function which allows you to continue to double a number continuously by hitting the equals sign. How many disciples would you have after the thirty-third multiplication?

If each disciple could help another person to become a disciple every six months, it would take only 16½ years to have more than 8.5 billion persons, a number well in excess of the world's estimated population in A.D. 2000. Although it is theoretically possible, this fact has not been proved in practice. Obviously, to reach the billions by multiplication, we must do it in a way other than those ways we presently use.

That brings us to the first critical point—to reproduce a disciple, one must be a disciple. Look at our demonstration exercise above. If the second disciple fails to reproduce, it cuts the final figure in half. Or suppose he is only half-hearted in learning and practices only one-half of what his discipler does. Then his disciple will pick up his half-hearted attitude and cut in half again the standards of the original disciple reducing them to one-fourth. The next generation will reduce them to one-eighth, and so on, until the original standards and teachings are inconsequential.

Satan seems to have a four-step strategy to sabotage God's plan. First, he blinds men to the gospel to prevent them from

believing in Christ. Second, he tempts new converts to keep them from obeying Christ and becoming true disciples. Third, he deceives and discourages disciples so they will not reproduce disciples. Fourth, he distracts disciple-makers and prevents them from training other disciple-makers.

BECOMING DISCIPLES

"Would you disciple me?" a young pastor asked. "I've been in a Baptist church since I was saved." He added, looking intently into my eyes, "I've graduated from seminary, but no one has ever discipled me."

PERSONAL LEARNING ACTIVITY 30
How about you? Can you pass the discipleship test below? Write yes or no in each blank after you have read the Scriptures.

_____ Read Luke 9:23. Are you denying yourself and taking up your cross daily?

_____ Read John 15:5. Is Jesus' life flowing through you?

_____ Read John 8:31. Are you demonstrating that you are his disciple by continuing to learn and to follow his teachings?

_____ Read John 13:34-35. Do people know you are his disciple by the way you love other Christians?

_____ Read John 15:8. Are you showing that you are Jesus' disciple by bearing spiritual fruit?

Jesus did not call people to be Christians but to be disciples. He did not tell them how easy it would be but how difficult. He did not invite them to walk an aisle but to follow him in daily obedience. He did not tell them to forget about the cost but to count it. However, Jesus did not require anyone to have certain talents, to be educated, or to be a member of a certain social class. He only demanded obedience. He took people wherever they were and led them to be more like him.

If we are to do the will of God on earth, we must recapture the life of discipleship as the norm in our churches. A disciple is one who makes Jesus Christ Lord of his life. He may fail in the application of his commitment at times, but there is no wavering in his allegiance to Christ as the Lord of his life.

Jesus said: "If any man come to me, and hate not his father, and mother, and wife, and children, and brethren, and sisters, yea, and his own life also, he cannot be my disciple. And whosoever doth not bear his cross, and come after me, cannot be my disciple" (Luke 14:26-27). How dare we lower the standards Jesus set for disciples? Do we have any right to invite anyone to follow Christ on terms less than those he set?

Would you like to become a better disciple? Here are four basic things a disciple does that you also can do.

Follow Jesus. When Jesus said, "Follow me," Peter, James, and John dropped what they were doing to go with him. They focused on Jesus as the guide of their lives and submitted to his leadership. They obeyed his commands. They conformed to his example. They did what they saw him doing.

One of the best disciples I know is a man who decided on the day he was converted that the commands of Jesus were true and binding on his life. Whenever he found a command in the Bible, he did his best to follow it. Unlike most of us, his life has not been a series of spiritual ups and downs but a continuous growth in Christlikeness.

Be an apprentice. "A horse will follow you a long way," a farmer once told me, "but to get any work out of him you have to put a bridle on him."

Jesus said, "Take my yoke upon you" (Matt. 11:29). He was speaking of a yoke that two oxen wore when they pulled a plow or a cart. Or he could have been referring to the rabbis who used this phrase to invite pupils to enter their schools. A disciple works alongside Jesus as an apprentice. He is concerned about the same things that Jesus is concerned about. He goes the same direction that Jesus is going. He is Jesus' partner and friend.

Be a learner. Jesus said, "Take my yoke upon you, and learn of me" (Matt. 11:29). One of the basic meanings of disciple is "learner." A disciple is always learning. To become a disciple means to enroll in the school of Christ and become involved in continuing education for the rest of your life.

Be a representative. "As my Father hath sent me, even so send I you," Jesus said to his disciples (John 20:21). Not only are you to be like Christ; you are to represent Christ! When someone is said to be a disciple of a famous educator or a psychologist, we expect him to represent his teacher truly. As a disciple, you have a responsibility to represent Christ in the unbelieving world.

To become biblical disciples we must follow the example of the Master Discipler.

Jesus: the Perfect Model for the Disciple

Perhaps you have never thought of Jesus modeling the role of a disciple on earth in his relationship with the Father. Remember, Jesus emptied himself when he came to earth and continually relied on the Father for everything. A study of John 5—7 will show how Jesus was the perfect model of a disciple.

PERSONAL LEARNING ACTIVITY 31
Read John 5:19-43 and list at least three ways Jesus modeled the behavior of a disciple by the way he responded to the Father.

Jesus did what he saw the Father doing, he did it in the same way, and he did it in the Father's power (John 5:19). Jesus did what the Father showed him (John 5:20). He was given all judgment, but he did not judge anything on his own initiative (John 5:22,30). He gave life to the dead as he received it of the Father (John 5:24-26). He came in his Father's name (John 5:43).

My applications of these verses include the following. Following Jesus' example, we should listen to God speak to us through his Word. We should look at what God is doing in the world and interpret daily events in the light of his purpose. Our evaluations and decisions should be made only after we consult with God. We should recognize that we can do nothing spiritual without him and, therefore, depend on him for life, love, wisdom, and power. We must be courageous enough to represent God, to seek only his honor, and to lead others to honor him.

PERSONAL LEARNING ACTIVITY 32
Read John 6:38-57 and write in your own words two ways Jesus identified his mission with the Father's.

Jesus' one purpose on earth was to do the Father's will instead of his own will (John 6:38). Jesus did not lose anyone the Father gave him. Rather, he discipled them (John 6:39). He received his life from the Father, and he passes it on to those who believe in him.

As we apply the lessons Jesus has taught us by example, our first priority should be to know and to do the will of the Father. To do that we must surrender our wills to him. We should follow up everyone whom God entrusts to our care and should do everything possible not to lose anyone. This responsibility of not losing the disciples committed to him probably made Jesus more patient. We should not expect our disciples to do better than Jesus', but neither should we expect to lose any that were drawn to Christ by the Father. Therefore, we must live in Christ. We must set the example of relying completely on God, rather than on our cleverness, tenacity, or discipline.

PERSONAL LEARNING ACTIVITY 33
Read John 7:16-28 and list two ways Jesus showed that his ministry was for the Father, not for himself.

Jesus taught the Father's teaching, not his own (John 7:16). He sought only the Father's glory (John 7:18). And he saw himself as the Father's representative (John 7:18).

All truth comes from God. We are only his representatives; and to be his representatives, we must have been with him and must have been sent by him. We must be obedient to learn. We must teach only his doctrine and glorify him. We need to quote the Father instead of quoting others or saying what we think. The wisdom of this world and the trends of the day distort the eternal truth. God is Teacher, Master, and Father; no representative should attempt to be the authority. Even Jesus did not. Jesus perfectly knew and taught God's way and is our living model of what God wants us to do.

Holy Spirit: the Perfect Model of a Servant

The Holy Spirit is part of the Godhead. But as we examine Jesus' teachings about the Holy Spirit and observe the Spirit related to Jesus, we realize that the Holy Spirit exemplifies the most important role of a disciple—that of a servant.

PERSONAL LEARNING ACTIVITY 34
Read Jesus' teachings about the Holy Spirit in the following passages: John 14:16; 16:13-15. Write two ways the Holy Spirit exemplifies the servant role.

Jesus promised another Comforter. The Greek word translated *another* carries the meaning of *one of the same kind.* The Holy Spirit is like Jesus. He acts and reacts like Jesus. He speaks only what he hears. He passes on to us what he receives from Jesus. He never glorifies himself but spotlights and honors Jesus. Jesus receives from the Father; the Spirit receives from the Son; we receive from the Spirit; and we are to pass it on to the rest of the world. The Holy Spirit exemplifies the true servant heart—the essence of being a disciple.

MAKING DISCIPLES

If we are to disciple men, we need to study how Jesus, the Master Disciple-builder, did it.

Model

The first prerequisite is to be an example of the behavior and attitudes you want your disciple to have. Jesus modeled this in his relationship with the Father. The pattern in Jesus' ministry was to do something before he taught it verbally. He reacted violently to the Pharisees, who "say, and do not" (Matt. 23:3). Discipling is not only correct doctrine; truth must be demonstrated in daily life.

Selection

Jesus prayed all night before he chose the twelve for special training (Luke 6:12). He chose ordinary men who had an extraordinary devotion to him. They would do anything he commanded them to do. Imagine what you would do if Jesus had commanded you to walk on the water . . . or catch a fish and pay the taxes with a coin found in its mouth . . . or borrow someone's colt without first asking the owner's permission. The disciples made many mistakes, yet obedience characterized their behavior.

Partnership

One essential ingredient in discipling is being with the disciple in all kinds of situations. Mark says, "He ordained twelve, that they should be with him, and that he might send them forth to preach" (Mark 3:14). The "with him" principle cannot be ignored. Since Jesus was to send them out as his representatives, they must have enough experience to act and to react as he would.

The nearer Christ came to the end of his earthly ministry, the more time he spent with his disciples. He poured himself into his men because they were the ones who would determine the scope of his future ministry.

The purpose of a discipler should be to share the secrets of his ministry. I once knew a plumber who would never tell his apprentice how to "wipe pipe," because it was a trade secret. The apprentice had to pick up the process for himself over a four- or five-year period. Jesus never hid his secrets from his disciples. Instead, he took his disciples aside and made sure they understood his teachings.

Life-Situation Learning

Jesus taught his disciples in the hustle and bustle of life. He never said, "In the morning at eight o'clock we will study 'Old Testament Prophecy' and at nine o'clock 'Modern Trends and Interpretation of the Torah.' " He lived with them twenty-four hours a day and used his own ministry as the primary reference point for teaching them. He used an incident, such as the rich young ruler who would not follow him, to teach about the relationship of possessions to the kingdom. On another occasion he prepared Philip for learning by telling him to feed the five thousand when they had no food. When the disciples' boat was tossed in the storm, they awoke him. Jesus immediately used the occasion to teach them a lesson. Jesus was always teaching them lessons from life that they could never forget.

Job-Related Training

Discipleship should always be linked to evangelism and ministry, or it will become sterile, ingrown, and ineffective.

Jesus sent out the twelve with only minimum instructions and limited responsibility, but he allowed them to learn on the job. At times, such as when he went to the mount of transfiguration, he left some of them behind to force them to serve. He followed up each assignment or task-related experience with explicit teaching.

Later Jesus sent out the seventy to learn on the job. Before he sent his disciples on their first mission, he demonstrated how they were to minister and gave them specific instructions. After they returned he talked with them and pointed out what he wanted them to learn from their experiences. Jesus planned for his disciples to be successful by preparing them ahead of time.

Jesus supervised the disciples' ministries to develop their character. He properly balanced love and rebuke, because they needed both to become disciple-makers. Delegation, without supervision and accountability, is abdication of responsibility.

GLOBAL DISCIPLESHIP

The phrase translated *go ye* in the Great Commission is a participle meaning *as you go* or *having gone*. Jesus assumed his disciples would go.

Going can be interpreted in two ways. First, as disciples went about their tasks in the world, they came in contact with people from many nations. Some even went to other countries for business or because of persecution. Through their ordinary life patterns disciples would reproduce other disciples who in turn would repeat the process and spread the good news in enlarging circles from Jerusalem, to Judea, to Samaria, and to the uttermost parts of the earth.

Second, disciples would go as missionaries to other cultures and nations. They were to go until they had made disciples of all nations. Jesus knew that the Holy Spirit would thrust them out. The universal nature of the gospel would cry in their hearts until they proclaimed it to all people. We find ourselves in a long chain of global discipleship.

Christ's mandate leaves no option. We are to make and to develop loyal disciples. The only imperative in the commission is, "Make disciples." Too often, we are satisfied with converts rather than disciples. Jesus never commanded us to engage in an evangelism that requires only mental assent. Nor did he expect us to take shortcuts in our haste to reach out. We should train new converts by taking them with us as we evangelize others. Both evangelism and discipleship can, and should, be done at the same time.

The second participle in Matthew 28:19, *baptizing*, relates the new disciple to Christ and his body, the church. Baptizing them is not an option either. If a person is not committed enough to Christ to be baptized after he has been instructed properly, he is not worthy to be Christ's disciple. People in many lands face ostracism, persecution, and even death when they are baptized in water, but Jesus said it should be done.

The third participle is *teaching*. I often ask people what Christ commanded us to teach. Almost invariably they will answer, "All things." Not so. He commanded us to teach them to "*observe* all things." He wants practice, not just doctrine. The word *observe* means to conform one's actions or practice to something. The job isn't finished when a person says yes to Christ. It has only begun. We must teach him to do Christ's commands.

REPRODUCING DISCIPLE-MAKERS

The discipling process comes alive in the vivid experiences of the main characters of the New Testament. Barnabas, nicknamed the son of encouragement, is one of the best examples. He probably trusted Christ at Pentecost and was discipled by one or more of the twelve.

Later he discipled Paul. When the apostles refused to have anything to do with Paul, Barnabas vouched for him, and they served together for a while in Jerusalem (Acts 9:23-29). Several years later Barnabas was sent to Antioch to help the young church during a great turning to Christ. Barnabas traveled an additional one hundred twenty miles to find Paul (Acts 11:25-26).

Barnabas continued to disciple Paul during the first phase of their ministry together in Antioch. Barnabas' name is always mentioned first. Only after they began their missionary journey does the order reverse to "Paul and Barnabas." Barnabas had led him until Paul surpassed his teacher. Barnabas' servant heart is revealed in his willingness to allow Paul to take the lead.

Later Barnabas discipled John Mark, even against Paul's advice, with the result that John Mark later wrote the Gospel of Mark. In the end Paul agreed that Mark was profitable to him (2 Tim. 4:11).

Paul followed Barnabas' example and chose Timothy as his disciple. Nearing death, Paul wrote Timothy, "The things that thou hast heard of me among many witnesses, the same commit thou to faithful men, who shall be able to teach others also" (2 Tim. 2:2).

The reproduction principle of discipling has now become clear in an ever growing chain of five generations. Barnabas discipled Paul, who discipled Timothy, who was to disciple a faithful man, who was able to teach others also. Reproducing disciples who will reproduce disciples is Christ's plan for world evangelization.

The local church is the proper arena for discipling. Jesus gave the Great Commission to the church. Because churches have neglected discipleship, groups outside the local churches have reclaimed the emphasis. But discipling outside the local church is out of context.

The church should be involved in three processes in its discipling ministry. First, the local body of believers wins converts and integrates them into the fellowship. Socialization occurs as the person adopts the attitudes and the patterns of the group. Few people who have been reared in a warm, evangelistic, nurturing local church realize how much their lives have been shaped by the behavior and attitudes of that church.

Second, the local church provides small groups that aid in internalization. Internalization is the process of incorporating a group's values and beliefs into one's own. Character formation takes place best in small-group interaction, such as in the family, in Sunday School, in Church Training, in missions organizations, and in special-interest groups. If a special small group covenants together to help one another become disciples and to hold one another accountable, it can be the most effective context for discipling. Small groups should be integrated into the local church program and add to its leadership.

Third, the local church should contain disciple-makers who can advance the process of multiplication. The multiplication of disciple-makers occurs mostly in one-to-one relationships between church leaders who have a vision of global discipleship and those who have already become disciples. It occurs when church leaders follow Jesus' example for making disciples.

I asked my grandfather, age ninety-six, and my grandmother, age eighty-nine, how many descendants they had. "Sixty-two," my grandmother answered quickly.

For fun I asked, "My, how did you raise them all?"

"I didn't raise them all, thank goodness," she exclaimed with a chuckle. "I just raised six of them."

"What about the rest?"

"Well, I helped some on the nineteen grandchildren; I helped some on you. But I didn't do much on the thirty-five great-grandchildren or the two great-great-grandchildren. Their parents took care of them."

Spiritual reproduction is God's mandate to mission.

BIBLIOGRAPHY

Coleman, Robert E. *Master Plan of Evangelism*. Old Tappan, N.J.: Fleming H. Revell, Co., 1978.

Eims, LeRoy. *The Lost Art of Disciple Making*. Grand Rapids: Zondervan Publishing House, 1978.

Hendrichsen, Walter A. *Disciples Are Made—Not Born*. Wheaton, Ill.: Victor Books, 1974.

Heunel, Albert. *The Humiliation of the Church*. Philadelphia: The Westminster Press, 1966.

How to Pray for Others. Equipping Center module. Nashville: The Sunday School Board of the Southern Baptist Convention, 1979.

How to Study Your Bible. Equipping Center module. Nashville: The Sunday School Board of the Southern Baptist Convention, 1979.

Wilson, Carl. *With Christ in the School of Disciple Building*. Grand Rapids: Zondervan Publishing House, 1976.

CHAPTER 7

Equipped for Mission

*"I remember seeing, at a circus, a man spinning
plates on eight sticks. He would just get all eight
going and have to run back to keep Number One
moving, and so on up the line. This seems to me
an apt illustration of the role of the pastor, who has
figured out the plates he wants to spin and looks
through the congregation to find the right sticks.
He gets it all going and discovers that the sticks
don't keep the plates moving, so he is stuck with
running up and down from plate to plate
operating programs which the sticks are not
motivated to spin."*[1]

A comparison of New Testament churches with the practices of
churches today makes us wonder if the following scenario might
not have taken place.

*Satan calls a summit meeting of the rulers of darkness,
the rulers of wickedness, the principalities, the powers, and
the demons sometime in the second half of the first century
A.D.*

*"I have called this extraordinary plenary session of rep-
resentatives from every sector of the Evil Kingdom because
we need a new strategy. Since the Pentecost sensation, we
have had a standoff or worse with the followers of the
Nazarene. Our strategy of intimidation, persecution, temptation, and murder has not stopped the church."*

"We have Paul, that over-zealous missionary, in jail,"
said the Spirit Prince of Rome, *"so we have their leadership
under wraps."*

"Remember Philippi!" warned the Spirit Prince of
Macedonia.

"Neither Paul nor the other leaders are our main problem," said Satan. "We have killed several of the apostles, but we can't stop the ordinary people."

"That's right," added the potentate of Palestine. "They talk about Jesus spontaneously, whether they have a leader or not. When we scatter them by persecution, it is like trying to stamp out a grass fire. In no time new leaders spring up."

"They don't need a place to meet either," added a demon from Asia Minor. "When we have them kicked out of synagogues or public meeting places, they just worship in their homes. When we have services banned, they go to the catacombs."

"Why should they be such a problem?" asked an evil spirit. "They are unlearned and ignorant."

"They may not be educated," said Legion, "but they are not unlearned in spiritual things. They can cast you out of somone in a moment. Their leaders equip and train them to face anything."

"Then how do we stop them?" asked Satan. "If we can't stop them by force, we must be shrewder."

All the evil spirit beings sat in silent despair. Suddenly Satan stood to his feet. "I have it!" he exclaimed. "We will make Christians think that only leaders can witness!"

"Hey, that's a great idea!" shouted the Spirit Prince of Greece. "We can tell them that leaders are different and no one else is equipped or ordained to do their jobs."

"And we can tell the leaders that they can have the authority in the church," said the Spirit Prince of Persia, "and they'll gladly fall for that!"

"Right!" said a spiritual potentate. "We can even tell them that the offices of the apostle, the prophet, the evangelist, and the teacher are all combined in the office of pastor. Then the pastor will have so much work to do that the church will hardly grow."

"That way," added the Spirit Prince of Persia, warming to the discussion, "he won't have time to pray or to study the Word."

"More important than that," Satan said, "he won't have time to equip the saints. Especially if we can keep him busy trying to do all the church's ministries."

"Then we can get the ordinary Christians to gripe at him because things aren't going well," added a demon, gleefully.

"We could even get them to say that the pastor gets paid to do the spiritual work," said the Spirit Prince of Egypt, "and the Christians will forget that they are priests, too. We can tell them they have nothing more to do than to support the pastor."

"Right," interjected a potentate, "and we could give the pastor designations to make him different. For instance, we could say he is 'full-time' so the members will think their ministry is 'part-time.' "

"We could say he is the servant of God so members would think they aren't. We could even say he has surrendered for special service so that they think their service isn't important."

"Then, if we could make him think he has special status through special spiritual gifts, ordination, or education," chipped in a lesser power, "we could wipe out the service of the people of God. They will think they are amateurs."

"We could even make them think that missionaries who go to other races are holier than anyone else. Then no ordinary Christian would ever dream he is to be a missionary," said the Spirit Prince of China.

Satan said: "Most honored potentates, principalities, powers, and demons, we have devised a most propitious strategy. It will take time to accomplish it, but it will work. We will revise our strategy and make Christianity respectable. That will dull the cutting edge and blur its distinctiveness to the world. We will convince men again, as we have in the past, that worship is to be done in a certain place and at a specific time. We will make them passive spectators of their hardworking leaders. Our kingdom will not be in danger if we can keep the church members passive and have to fight only overburdened leaders."

History documents the taming of the church whether this
scenario happened or not. A growing hierarchical system separated the clergy from the laity. The church began to assume that
spiritual gifts were given only to the clergy and that where the
bishop was there was the church. By A.D. 312 Christianity had
become the official religion of Rome. Constantine made it popu-
lar to be a Christian. Men who wanted to live pure lives became
monks. The monastery was considered the place for a pure
Christian life, while the masses had to live in the world and
become a part of it. Christianity entered the Dark Ages for a
thousand years. Although the faithful rejected these trends and
followed the Bible, they were too few to stem the tide.

Luther attempted to reinstate New Testament principles but
fell short. He championed the priesthood of the believers re-
garding individual access to God but failed to carry the doctrine
to its logical conclusion. Snyder says:

The presbyterian and congregational systems arising
from the Reformation brought some practical im-
provements, but both systems rested on many an un-
tested Roman Catholic assumption about the essential
nature of the church. This is evident particularly in the
doctrine of spiritual gifts and the general concept of
ministry, where the Roman Catholic clergy-laity
dichotomy was largely carried over.[2]

Baptists were called radicals during the Reformation because, among other things, they practiced the freedom and the
responsibility of each believer to minister. However, as the
centuries have passed, Baptist practices often have belied our
theology.

Howard E. Butt, Jr., a noted lay leader, spoke at a breakfast I attended just before our family went to Indonesia as missionaries. He said: "In practice, Baptists have developed a pyramid-shaped hierarchy, with the laymen on the bottom. They are to support the church leaders by attending services, helping do the church work, and giving. On the next level are the music directors. Above them are the educational directors. Near the top are the pastors. On the very top of the pyramid is the missionary . . . to Indonesia."

After he finished speaking, I told him, "I am a new missionary on my way to Indonesia!" He laughed. We both agreed that God has no such hierarchy.

WHO ARE THE SOLDIERS?

Thus far in this book we have examined the spiritual warfare between the kingdom of God and the kingdom of evil. The time has come to ask: Who are the soldiers? What is the job of the generals? Are the pastors, the teachers, the evangelists, the preachers, and the missionaries to fight the battle on the front

lines while the laymen just send more ammunition and pray for them? Have we slipped so far from the priesthood of the believers that only the ordained are qualified to fight? Have we elevated the ministry so high that only those with certain educational qualifications need apply? Have the laymen gladly accepted subordinate roles so that they will not be required to live up to the New Testament teaching about ministry? Is it easier to hire someone to fight for us?

The battle rages; and although the number of Christian soldiers increases, their ratio to nonbelievers decreases. The field is the world, and the people of God live in that world every day. More than three billion people in the world today do not follow Christ. The New Testament reveals both the message and the methods to accomplish God's plan for getting the gospel to every person. This chapter addresses the first half of the problem—the role of God-appointed leadership. The next chapter will explore the corollary truth of the ministry of all the people of God. The people of God will never be able to perform their ministries until they are equipped.

GOD APPOINTS LEADERS TO EQUIP HIS PEOPLE FOR MISSION

Ephesians 4:1-16 describes both God's purpose for his church and the means to accomplish it. In addition to teaching that every member has a calling and a spiritual gift, the passage says that Christ endowed the church with certain persons whose duty it is to equip the saints. "These were his gifts: some to be apostles, some prophets, some evangelists, some pastors and teachers, to equip God's people for work in his service, to the building up of the body of Christ" (Eph. 4:11-12, NEB).

The Greek word translated *equip* or *perfect* in verse 12, means to *mend*. It can mean to mend a net, to set a broken bone, to put a person in a right place or condition, or to restore a fallen church member. It also can mean to educate, to train, to guide, or to enable a person fully to do a task. The equipper's task is to perfect the saints so that they can do the work of the ministry and build up the body of Christ.

Translators of the King James Version incorrectly inserted a comma after the first clause in verse 12, making all three clauses seem to be the work of the equippers. (The original manuscripts had no punctuation.) But in the Greek a different word for *for* meaning *in order that* clearly shows that it is the saints who are to do the work of the ministry.

PERSONAL LEARNING ACTIVITY 36
Read Ephesians 4:12. Note how it reads in the following translations. Then paraphrase the verse.
1. "With a view to the fitting of the saints for the work of ministering . . ." (*The Emphasized New Testament*).[3]
2. "In order fully to equip His people for the work of serving . . ." (Weymouth).[4]
3. "For the immediate equipment of God's people for the work of service . . ." (Williams).[5]
4. "In order to get His holy people ready to serve as workers . . ." (Beck).[6]

The primary purpose of the equippers is to enable the saints to minister. Each equipper functions in the area of ministry that God has appointed to him (apostle, prophet, evangelist, or pastor-teacher). However, his ultimate goal of building up the church depends on his equipping the saints to minister in that particular area.

What are they to equip the saints to do? First, to walk worthy of their calling (Eph. 4:1). The word *vocation* in this verse is a translation of the word *calling*. The equippers implement God's call to the saints by helping them live worthy lives of humility, meekness, long-suffering, forbearance, and unity (Eph. 1:18; 4:1-6).

Second, they equip the saints for ministry. They help them understand their gifts (Eph. 4:7) and prepare them for service and witness.

Third, they equip the saints to build up the body of Christ. The word translated *build up* means to construct a building. A building should be built with quality materials and should be large enough to accommodate the purposes of the owner. The saints, as well as the equippers, build up both the size and the quality of the body of Christ.

Each equipper has a ministry to perform and to model while he is equipping the saints. Look at each ministry.

Apostle

The word *apostle* means *one who is sent* and is used for others in addition to the original twelve. Today he is the missionary to new areas. Paul gave us the best example of the apostolic function. An apostle goes to virgin territory, reaches people for Christ, plants churches, helps them grow, and then moves on. The apostle equips the church for its missionary function by his example, his reporting, his exhortation, and his training of others for missionary service.

Prophet

The prophet proclaims God's word and concern about nations, churches, and individuals. He primarily speaks to God's people

to call them back to God's mission. He exposes sin and injustice and pronounces God's judgment on those who refuse to follow God's ways. He builds up the church by edifying, by exhorting, and by comforting its members (1 Cor. 14:3). Even when Christians refuse to allow themselves to be equipped, the prophet does, in fact, equip the church with a holy value system, a sense of justice, and an urgency for the coming kingdom. He reveals God's work in this present age. His primary function is "forthtelling," although prophets sometimes "foretell" future events. The prophet proclaims the truth and exhorts the people of God to repent and to return to biblical norms.

Evangelist

The evangelist proclaims the good news to the lost, both to masses and to individuals. He has a special ability to help people make decisions for Christ. His ministry keeps him on the cutting edge between the church and the world. He goes to the world to tell the good news; he relates to the church to bring the newly converted to the body of Christ and to equip all God's children to witness.

The apostle, the prophet, and the evangelist often move throughout the churches. Like cells in the bloodstream, they bring life and cleansing to the body. They model and sharpen the ministries of local members of the body who have these same functions.

Pastor-Teacher

The Greek construction of Ephesians 4:11 links the pastor and teacher in a single ministry. The pastor-teacher ministers primarily in a local congregation and needs to stay long enough to teach and to train God's children. He nurtures the young and the weak in the faith, builds up the church, and equips each member of the body to fulfill his particular ministry. Other passages list the teacher separately, but the emphasis here is that the pastor must be apt to teach. He trains Christians to minister instead of trying to do it all himself.

Apostles and evangelists primarily emphasize building up

the church by adding new churches and new converts. Prophets and pastor-teachers usually emphasize building up the quality of the church. The saints build up the church in both ways because they are fitted properly for their dual role in the body and in the world.

RETURN TO THE BIBLICAL PRINCIPLE

Again, we must ask the question, Who are the soldiers? Can you imagine generals attacking the enemy by themselves while the troops only cheer them on and supply the ammunition? Can you imagine a football coach playing the opposing team in the Super Bowl while the players lead the spectators in cheers? It is just as absurd for us to expect the equippers alone to defeat Satan and the world.

The analogy of the equipper as a coach is misunderstood often because most of us picture the coach on the sidelines urging his team on and sending in the plays. But the coach's primary job is training his players during the week. He gets on the practice field with them and shows them how to block, tackle, and run. He praises them when they do well and corrects their mistakes. He loves them and the game. The players seek to follow his example and his instructions.

Now compare our modern practice with the biblical teaching. Modern church practice has reduced all the equipping ministers to one—the pastor. A few exceptional pastors may be able to fulfill these roles as a performer, but one pastor cannot adequately equip all members of the body in these four functions. The New Testament teaches a plurality of elders (pastors) in a local church (Acts 4:23; 15:2; 20:17; 1 Thess. 1:5; Jas. 5:14; 1 Pet. 5:1).

We demand that pastors do the jobs of several men. In addition, we require them to perform the ministry of the entire church. Furthermore, we add extrabiblical duties that have grown out of our culture. Something must be done; we are killing our pastors.

"But only a few churches could support all the equippers," you say. True, unless you take the biblical model of many bivocational or unpaid equippers. The gospel will never be heard by every person if we must depend only on a specialized, paid ministry to evangelize them. Those we do support must equip the rest to minister. Those we cannot support must minister because they were appointed by Christ, even though they may have to make tents for a living.

PERSONAL LEARNING ACTIVITY 37
List two practical ways that you think would help us return to a biblical model for the equipping ministries.

We can return to the biblical pattern by upholding the biblical ideal rather than an ecclesiastical one inherited from other churches. We can affirm that not all equippers must be supported financially by a local church but may receive their support from a number of churches or from other jobs.

A pastor can recognize which of the equipping ministries he has been given by Christ and major on it. Then he can enlist those from the congregation (or from outside it) to perform the missionary, the evangelistic, the pastoral, or the prophetic equipping ministries he has not been appointed to do. We can insist that equippers make equipping the saints their first priority.

On a wider plane, we can recognize and can utilize the equipping ministry of associational missionaries who may perform one or more of the equipping functions. Our churches can use the equipping ministries of evangelists, teachers, prophets, and denominational workers whose ministries are to many churches instead of primarily to one local church. We can educate our people in churches, in colleges, and in seminaries about the equipping ministries.

On the international front, we can help missionaries identify their particular equipping functions and concentrate on them. Missionaries should teach nationals the biblical pattern and enable them to be equippers. If churches in other lands are to reach the millions around them, a large number of their pastors must be bivocational. Even in the United States more than nine thousand Baptist pastors also work in secular jobs.

Clearly, we are not downgrading the pastors but lifting them to the ministry to which God has appointed them. As they perform their basic function of equipping, the church will be able to minister and to grow.

Before the church can fulfill its ministry, both sides of the problem must be dealt with. Leaders must concentrate on performing their equipping ministries, and the people of God must accept their role as ministers who need to be equipped.

Five months before Vietnam fell to the Communists, I was asked to lead a missionary prayer retreat at Dalat, Vietnam. God sent a spiritual awakening. Missionaries confessed their sins, righted wrongs with one another, and had their needs met by the Lord. Prayer continued far into the night. One missionary was instantaneously healed as the group prayed for her.

I shared with them the biblical concepts of the equipping ministries, and they responded: "If this is true, then we have gone about our work the wrong way. We should determine whom God has appointed as apostles, as prophets, as evangelists, as pastors, and as teachers and then work together in a team approach."

No one had any indication that the South Vietnamese government would collapse so quickly. Nevertheless, they organized teams to minister according to the gifts and appointments of God. Teams went into new areas with each member concentrating on his specialty. Churches were crowded beyond capacity, and new ones were begun. Evangelists preached, and crowds of people accepted Christ. Teachers taught the basics of the Christian life to these new Christians. Then they equipped local church leaders to lead and to develop these churches. Hundreds came to Christ in those few months.

Little news about these Christians and churches has leaked out of Vietnam since its fall, but word has come that under adverse conditions many still are functioning because they were equipped to do their jobs.

NOTES

1. John MacArthur, Jr., *The Church: the Body of Christ* (Grand Rapids: Zondervan Publishing House, 1973), p. 124. Used by permission.
2. Howard A. Snyder, *The Problem of Wine Skins* (Downers Grove, Ill.: Inter-Varsity Press, 1976), p. 52. Used by permission.
3. From *The Emphasized New Testament* by Joseph Bryant Rotherham (Grand Rapids: Kregel Publications).
4. From *Weymouth's New Testament in Modern Speech* by Richard Francis Weymouth, published by special arrangement with James Clarke and Company, Ltd., and reprinted by permission of Harper & Row, Publishers, Inc.
5. From *The New Testament, a Translation in the Language of the People* by Charles B. Williams. Copyright 1937 and 1966. Moody Press, Moody Bible Institute of Chicago.
6. From *The Holy Bible in the Language of Today* by William F. Beck. Copyright © Mrs. William F. Beck, 1976. Published by A. J. Holman Company. Used by permission of the publisher.

BIBLIOGRAPHY

Come, Arnold B. *Agents of Reconciliation.* Philadelphia: The Westminster Press, 1969.
Discovering Your Spiritual Gifts. Equipping Center module. Nashville: The Sunday School Board of the Southern Baptist Convention, 1981. (Available July 1981)
Harkness, Georgia. *The Church and Its Laity.* Nashville: Abingdon Press, 1962.
Kraemer, Hendrik. *A Theology of the Laity.* Philadelphia: The Westminster Press, 1958.
Moore, William J. *New Testament Concept of the Ministry.* St. Louis: Bethany Press, 1956.
Weltage, Ralph. *The Church Swept Out.* Boston: United Church Press, 1967.

CHAPTER 8

The People of God on Mission

*God's people should be evaluated on the basis of
their faith, ability to bear responsibility, and the
exercise of spiritual gifts in their ministries, not on
factors that have arisen in history to divide them
into classes, such as status (clergy or laity), money
(paid or voluntary), education (general or
theological), time (full-time or part-time), or
calling (specific or general).*

Use your imagination again to step back into the first century to
see the people of God on mission.

"Thank you, Aquila and Priscilla, for welcoming us into
your home. We've heard of the phenomenal growth of the
churches in Asia and would like to see yours."

"We are glad to have you, but it will be rather difficult
for you to see our church. It is scattered all over town and
throughout the provinces, wherever the disciples are."

"You mean you have no buildings?"

"We meet in homes like this one for worship and for
fellowship."

"But how can you grow a church in such a small
house?"

"We can't help but grow. Every week we have to start
new churches in homes to meet the demand. As soon as
disciples are equipped, they begin new churches."

"But couldn't you evangelize your city faster if you had
your own building? Lost people would be attracted to it, and
the community would respect you more."

"We already have more attention than we want since the riot caused by the silversmiths. Besides, we've already taken the gospel to every person in Asia."

"Everyone in Asia! That's impossible! You mean all the Jews and Greeks in Ephesus, in Smyrna, in Colosse, in Sardis, on up into Bithynia, and out to Cappadocia?"

"Sure. And many other places, too. Priscilla and I are planning to move to Rome soon to start a church in our home there as a beachhead for evangelizing the whole Roman Empire. Paul plans to go to Spain, and other disciples are moving to Alexandria and to North Africa."

"How in the world did you do it?"

"Asia was not nearly so difficult as the rest of the world will be, but the plan is quite simple. We are tentmakers, as you can see. That's how we met our friend Paul in Corinth. He introduced us to the Lord. Since then, we've just followed the pattern of the first church in Jerusalem. Paul brought us to Ephesus when he went to Jerusalem on his second tour. We made some disciples and counseled others, like Apollos. But the job wasn't finished until Paul returned and led twelve of Apollos' disciples to Christ and baptized them. He taught them about the Holy Spirit, and things haven't been the same around here since."

"If churches here at Ephesus were started by them in their homes, didn't you have many doctrinal errors and divisions?"

"Not many. Paul taught us for two years in the school of Tyrannus while we were evangelizing Asia and beginning churches."

"You mean that Paul left after two years? How could he do that?"

"Well, he actually stayed three years, but he felt his work of equipping us had been finished. Being an apostle, he wanted to go preach the gospel where no one else had been."

"What did you do for a pastor?"

"Paul appointed several elders, like myself, and helped

us understand our ministries as apostles, as prophets, as evangelists, as pastors, and as teachers. We concentrate on equipping all the disciples to minister."

"You mean that all of you are ministers?"

"Yes, in our own way. How else could we have evangelized so many in Asia? We each use our spiritual gifts to serve the Lord. We have gone from house to house testifying and teaching the Truth. We've also had a few public meetings."

"How did you get everyone to minister?"

"From the first day Paul came to Asia, he wept and testified everywhere. He was determined that no person would be lost because he had neglected his responsibility. We have caught his vision."

"This is amazing! Let us ask you one more question. Is each disciple a leader?"

"Of course not. God gives many kinds of spiritual gifts. Each gift supports the others. A person with a gift of mercy is as important to the church as one who has a gift of administration. Each of us ministers in the area of his spiritual gifts. It appears that much of this is strange to you. Is what we are doing unusual? Do you have any new ways that might help us get the gospel to every person before the Lord returns or before our generation passes?"

"We have some new and modern means, but you have given us something much more valuable. Thank you for letting us visit in your home. You'll never know how much your example can help us finish the job God has given us to do."

PERSONAL LEARNING ACTIVITY 38
Read the passages listed which tell about the events mentioned above. Then list any three important biblical principles of missions in action in the first century. Acts 18:18-21; 19:8-10; 20:17-35; Romans 16:3.

EVERY BELIEVER IS A MINISTER

Not only does the church involve the laity; it is the laity. The word *laity* comes from the Greek word *laos* and means simply *people*. The Septuagint version of the Old Testament uses this word over two thousand times for the people of God. The New Testament uses it one hundred forty times for the church as God's people.[1]

The word *clergy* is derived from the Greek word *kleros*, which means *heritage*. It means all of God's people, as in 1 Peter 5:3, "Neither as being lords over God's *heritage*." In 2 Corinthians 6:16, *kleros* has the same meaning as *laos*.

Therefore, the biblical, meaning of *laos* and *kleros* includes all of God's people and does not make a distinction between laity and clergy.

Our modern usage of the terms is derived from the Graeco-Roman political situation rather than from the Bible. The Roman government was divided between the *kleros*, who were trained, powerful magistrates, and the *laos*, who were ignorant, uneducated peasants.

> . . . in Western culture . . . "lay" came to indicate the mass of the uninformed (in any field) who are incapable of making responsible judgments or of acting with authority.
>
> Nothing could be further from the Biblical idea of God's chosen *laos*. His people have been called into being out of the mass of humanity, and the people as a whole are distinguished by their knowledge of God and their power to do his will.[2]

Baptists traditionally have resisted the idea of a distinction between *clergy* and *laity*. Nevertheless, the philosophy and practice have crept into our churches. Some even feel that church members should be like assistant pastors who are to help pastors get the work done. The Bible teaches that as equippers, the pastors are servants who should train the people of God so the people themselves get the work done.

Another biblical term that has acquired a new meaning in modern usage is the word *call*. This is the translation of a Greek word, *kaleo,* used in the New Testament to refer to those who have been *called* by God and who have listened to his voice addressed to them in the gospel, hence those who have enlisted in the service of Christ.[3]

Today we use *call* in a special sense, such as "called to be a preacher," "called to be a missionary," "called to a church." This elevates the call of part of God's people over the call of the rest of God's people. In the New Testament, God's call is his act of electing and marking off an entire people for his special purpose.

Jesus called men to a new way of life. He demanded their complete dedication before he would allow them to become his followers. The call to discipleship is the call to devote all that one has and is to Christ as Lord. Any other service is a part of that call, not a higher call. One cannot surrender more than everything. Jesus turned away those who gave first allegiance to possessions, to family, or to position. We must not downgrade a part of the body of Christ to elevate another part.

PERSONAL LEARNING ACTIVITY 39
Read the following Scriptures and note the meaning of the word *call.* Where you think it applies to all believers write yes. Where you think it applies to only a special class of ministers write no.

1. 1 Corinthians 1:16 _____

2. Ephesians 1:18 _____

3. Ephesians 4:17 _____

4. 2 Thessalonians 1:11 _____

5. 2 Timothy 1:9 _____

Findley Edge said: "The call to salvation and the call to ministry is one and the same call. That is, when one is called by God to be a part of his people, he is also called into the ministry."[4]

Every believer is called to perform a ministry. Each member of the body has been called to build up the body so that we

. . . may grow up into him in all things, who is the head, even Christ: from whom the whole body fitly joined together and compacted by that which *every* joint supplieth, according to the effectual working in the measure of *every* part, maketh increase of the body unto the edifying of itself in love (Eph. 4:15-16).

Arnold B. Come said:

Whenever a particular formation of the church's ministerial functions fails any longer to impart to the whole membership a sense of mission to the world, then that formation lies under the judgment of God. The time for *reformation* is at hand.[5]

EVERY BELIEVER HAS A SPIRITUAL GIFT

God has given each Christian one or more spiritual gifts (1 Cor. 12:7; Rom 12:4-6; Eph. 4:7; 1 Pet. 4:10). These gifts enable him to minister in the power of the Spirit alongside other Christians who minister with their gifts.

Spiritual gifts are abilities given to men by the Holy Spirit to be manifested in his service for the good of other people.

PERSONAL LEARNING ACTIVITY 40

A definition of spiritual gifts comes from the five Greek words in 1 Corinthians 12:1-7. Read the passage and the definitions and write your own definition of a spiritual gift.

Pneumatikon (v. 1) literally means the spirituals. The word *gift* is not used although it is understood.

Charismaton (v. 4) means *grace gift,* that is, something which is given based on the love of the giver, not the merit of the one who receives the gift.

Diakonion (v. 5) means *service* or ministry.

Energematon (v. 6) means *energizings* or bursts of power.

Phanerosis (v. 7) means *manifestations* or *evidences.*

Now write in your own words a definition of spiritual gifts.

Spiritual (*pneumatikon*) _____(*charismaton*) are

abilities or _____(*energematon*) given to

a person by Christ to be _____

(*phanerosis*) in his _____

(*diakonion*) for the good of other people.

The correct words are defined above in the following order: verses 1,4,6,7,5.

In summary, spiritual gifts are abilities or powers given to a person by the Holy Spirit to be manifested in his service for the good of other people.

As the people of God we no longer can ignore the spiritual gifts that equip God's people to minister. Interpretations differ as to how many gifts there are, which ones are operative today, and what evidences show that one has a certain spiritual gift.

PERSONAL LEARNING ACTIVITY 41
Read Romans 12:4-8; 1 Corinthians 12:8-11,28-30; Ephesians 4:7-11; and 1 Peter 4:10-11. List the spiritual gifts that you believe God gives.

One list includes prophecy, service (helps), teaching, exhortation, giving, administration (ruling), mercy, word of wisdom, word of knowledge, faith, healing, miracles, discerning of spirits, tongues, interpretation of tongues, apostolic (missionary) gift, evangelism, and shepherding.

Each Christian should know his gift(s) and allow the Spirit to develop it(them). The certainty that one has a gift comes as he serves God, develops the abilities he has, and is sensitive to the Holy Spirit who distributes and affirms his gifts.

Spiritual gifts are not merit badges given for holiness or effort. They are spiritual abilities given to persons to enable them to minister to the entire body (1 Cor. 12:11-18,25). Spiritual gifts are not to call attention to themselves or to be used for personal benefit. They are to point to Christ, his presence and power. Some in the church at Corinth thought that a particular gift was for the exclusive benefit of the individual. Such a belief denies the function of the body (1 Cor. 12:25). Even the body of Christ does not function for its own good but for Christ and the world. Spiritual gifts are always to be used under the guidance of the Spirit *and* the local congregation to avoid the errors of the Corinthian church.

The fruit of the Spirit expresses the new spiritual nature. Paul identified the fruit of the spirit as love, joy, peace, longsuffering, gentleness, goodness, faith, meekness, and temperance (Gal. 5:22-23). A life that has these qualities is the kind of life in which spiritual gifts can flourish.

The best evidence of a Spirit-led life is the presence of the fruit of the Spirit. All Christians should have all nine expressions of the fruit (singular) of the Spirit. Not all Christians have all the gifts (plural). In fact, it would be exceptional if one had all the gifts, since one purpose of the differing gifts is to bind all Christians into one interdependent body (1 Cor. 12:11-27). Specific instructions are given to prevent the misuse of the gifts (1 Cor. 12—14). If the gifts are functioning properly in the body of Christ, the church will be built up, and Christ's ministry to the world will be performed.

Spiritual gifts are given by God, not chosen by Christians. The Holy Spirit gives them to individuals according to his will (1 Cor. 12:11,18). God determines the gift(s) you have and the ministry you perform. You are not to covet another's gift or look down on your own. First Corinthians 14 emphasizes that the best gifts for you are the ones that make it possible for you to have the widest ministry to others. The Bible does not teach that a person can choose his own gift or that everyone must have a certain gift (such as tongues). If you have a particular gift, you have no reason to be proud; or if you do not have a particular gift, you need not be embarrassed. God decides.

Spiritual gifts differ from the fruit of the Spirit and from talents. Talents are endowments from God given at birth; spiritual gifts are endowments given at spiritual birth.

PERSONAL LEARNING ACTIVITY 42
Match the following distinctives of gifts, talents, and fruit by drawing a line between the correct relationships. (Note that some may fit more than one category, but try to identify the most precise relationship.)

IN ORIGIN:
1. Gifts   *a.* Physical abilities
2. Talents   *b.* Spiritual qualities
3. Fruit   *c.* Spiritual abilities

IN USE:
1. Gifts   *a.* Primarily for the benefit of Christ and his body
2. Talents   *b.* Primarily for benefit of others
3. Fruit   *c.* Primarily for benefit of self or of others

IN NUMBER:
1. Gifts   *a.* Nine
2. Talents   *b.* Unlimited
3. Fruit   *c.* Limited

IN OPERATION:
1. Gifts   *a.* Operated by self
2. Talents   *b.* Operated by the power of the Holy Spirit
3. Fruit   *c.* Operated by the presence of the Holy Spirit

I answered as follows: ORIGIN: 1-*c*, 2-*a*, 3-*b*; USE: 1-*a*, 2-*c*, 3-*b*; NUMBER: 1-*c*, 2-*b*, 3-*a*; OPERATION: 1-*b*, 2-*a*, 3-*c*.

Spiritual gifts may be developed or misused. Paul urged Timothy to stir up his gift (2 Tim. 1:6). If you identify your gift(s), you can use and develop it (them) better. The gift resides in you by the grace of the Holy Spirit, and he endeavors to develop and to refine you to maximum usefulness. Spiritual gifts may be misused, also. Misuse of gifts shows immaturity. You need to be sure that you are filled and led of the Spirit to avoid excesses (Eph. 5:18).

Satan, as usual, attempts to counterfeit what God does, and you need to be on guard lest he deceive you into exercising your gift(s) in the flesh. Test also the spirit of others lest they deceive you (1 John 4:1-2). Do not be surprised that Satan attempts to discredit the Holy Spirit. And do not allow him to confuse you or to cause you to shy away from God, the Holy Spirit, his gifts, and his ministry.

The presence of a spiritual gift proves that God has given you a spiritual ability to minister. The gifts function best in connection with the fruit of the Spirit, especially love. Talents should be surrendered to God for his complete use in the kingdom. Let your ministry flow out of your spiritual gifts. Your spiritual gift(s) may be expressed through a talent if you are surrendered to God and let the Holy Spirit guide you.

EVERY BELIEVER EXTENDS THE BODY TO THE WORLD

Early churches grew because they served in the world. They worshiped and ministered in homes. (See Matt. 8:14-15; 9:23-24; Mark 2:15-17; Luke 10:5-7; Acts 2:2-4,46; 5:42; 10:24-48; 20:20; 21:8-14; 28:30-31; Rom. 16:3-5; Col. 4:15; Philem. 2; Jas. 5:14-16.) The "house church" is making a comeback in Korea, in Brazil, in Chile, in Africa, in Indonesia, in America, and in other countries. It is the only kind of church that has survived in some Communist areas.

I talked with the pastor from Seoul, Korea, whose church had grown to fifty thousand members in ten years and is adding a thousand people a month. He said: "One secret of our growth is twenty-six hundred cell groups that meet in homes under the leadership of church members. Evangelism is automatic now. It happens so easily because the cells are working. If each cell adds only one family, that is over two thousand families. On Sunday they come to the church building. Our auditorium holds only eight thousand, so we have many services to take care of about forty-five thousand who attend."

The New Testament practice of using homes for worship has many advantages. Unsaved persons who seldom attend church services or revivals can be reached often by small groups in homes or in apartment complexes. A warm Bible study in a Christian home appeals to many in our alienated, lonely society. Services in homes allow each ethnic or social group to worship and to take their first steps toward Christ without having to cross natural barriers. Church growth is not limited by the space available in church buildings or by particular times of the week.

In home meetings evangelism becomes a more natural part of an individual's life as he worships and functions in society. Each person can minister more easily according to his spiritual gifts in the nurture and the interaction of a small group that aids in the maturing of Christians. These groups can be feeders for the corporate worship services of the entire local congregation or can create new ones as they expand.

Churches in America and around the world should consider this New Testament practice before problems such as the energy shortage, taxation of church property, government restrictions that could come with political change, and lawlessness force them to it. Practical experience in house churches would equip Christians to begin new churches when they move to unchurched areas. Missionaries could have field experience before going to other nationalities or countries. In many countries the only way left to begin churches that grow out of and that thrive in the environment is the church in the home.

If this method seems too radical, remember that Sunday School first began in homes. One of the reasons Baptists and Methodists outgrew other denominations on the American frontier was that they met in homes and in schools, as well as in church buildings. They were led by their local leaders.

New Testament churches grew in ever widening circles. As

Christians witnessed, people responded and new churches were started. The local church is God's plan for missions. Reproducing disciples multiply churches. As churches grow and multiply, they become advance stations for world evangelization. Churches can extend their witness to the world through cooperative efforts in associations, conventions, and agencies. Modern-day examples can be seen in the way Baptist churches, associations, state conventions, and the Home Mission Board combine their efforts to extend the kingdom.

In 1965, while Watts was still burning after massive riots and looting, Jack O'Neal, California director of Cooperative Ministries with National Baptists, called E. V. Hill, a prominent National Baptist pastor in Watts. "Ed," he said, "I'm watching all this on TV. What can we as Southern Baptists do?"

One thing they tried was saturating the area with the gospel, and they started through Vacation Bible Schools.

Hill's church, Mt. Zion, sponsored four Vacation Bible Schools the next summer; the Home Mission Board sent two summer missionaries to help.

In 1967, Mt. Zion sponsored ten Vacation Bible Schools, and the Board sent four student missionaries.

In 1968, Mt. Zion had eighty-two Vacation Bible Schools which reached six thousand people.

Out of this flurry of activity came the idea for the twin-triplet program. Sid Smith came to Los Angeles in September 1968. He wanted to extend Vacation Bible Schools into backyards, garages, or wherever he and the churches could find a spot to meet.

In 1969, five area churches had ten Vacation Bible Schools each. In 1970, the element of twinning was added, pairing three white churches with three black churches. In 1971, Smith expanded that to the triplet program, bringing in Spanish churches.

In 1974, a dozen churches, including a Chinese church, cooperated in triplet or twin programs. Each team of churches has to hold at least ten Vacation Bible Schools. "Many have never held more than one Vacation Bible School," Smith said.

"At first, they say: 'Naw, ten? We can't do ten.' But they do."

By 1978, 25,000 had attended Vacation Bible School, and 2,000 professions of faith had been made.[6]

Associations initiate many kinds of mission projects to help Christians to extend the body of Christ. Associational projects in Arkansas in 1979 included such ministries as administering disaster relief funds to tornado victims, sponsoring a joint revival crusade of Southern Baptist and National Baptist churches, establishing a mission Sunday School in a mountain community, beginning a new mission using a portable chapel building owned by an association, developing a broad ministry to Hispanic migrants, and ministering to Vietnamese and Laotian immigrants.[7]

The state conventions cooperate with the Home Mission Board to extend the kingdom across natural and ethnic barriers. In the city of Los Angeles alone Baptists have established churches among twenty-three different language groups.

First-century Christians crisscrossed the nations of the known world as businessmen, as tourists, as soldiers, as explorers, as students, and so on, but "they that were scattered abroad went every where preaching the word" (Acts 8:4). They went for many reasons but with one purpose—the spreading of the gospel. When Christians recognize their call, develop their gifts, and engage in missions in their natural surroundings, they will minister to people of other nationalities as they go (Matt. 28:19).

God calls missionaries out of growing, spiritual churches to go to the uttermost parts of the earth. The first fruit of missions, the church at Antioch, sent their two best equippers to other nations.

As they ministered to the Lord, and fasted, the Holy Ghost said, Separate me Barnabas and Saul for the work whereunto I have called them. And when they had fasted and prayed, and laid their hands on them, they sent them away (Acts 13:2-3).

The Antioch church furnishes us a model for sending missionaries. First, they spent time in fasting and in prayer, thereby

127

placing themselves in position to hear God speak. Second, they sent their best equippers. Third, they cooperated with the Holy Spirit to send missionaries. (Acts 13:3 says the church sent them; verse 4 says the Spirit sent them.) Fourth, they commended them to the grace of God for mission work. Fifth, they received reports of the fulfilled ministries of the missionaries (Acts 14:26-27). Sixth, they commanded them to return for further missionary service (Acts 15:40).

Extending the kingdom to all people will require sending out tens of thousands of missionaries. Two billion of the three billion persons who are not Christians live in an environment where there are no known Christians. This means they will not hear the gospel until someone has crossed cultural and communication barriers. Every country in the world is made up of a widely varied mix of people—tribes, castes, occupational groups, language groups, religious groups, and combinations of these. Some estimates identify over 15,000 such groups in 221 countries of the world.[8]

Missionaries must impart to their converts the spirit of missions that brought them as missionaries, or they will forge dead-end links in God's chain of purpose. Any Christian or any church that is not missionary is out of the will of God. Nonmissionary churches are too immature to think beyond their own needs to the needs of others, are ignorant of God's purpose, or are disobedient to their Lord.

In the people-packed harbor area of Jakarta, Indonesia, thrives an unusual church that bears a close resemblance to New Testament churches. After the pastor moved to another church several years ago, the members began to lead the services. Thirteen of them study in the Indonesian Baptist Theological Seminary's extension program which trains them as they serve. In time the church began satellite churches in five homes to reach non-Christians during the week. On Sunday they attend the services at the mother church. A dockworker, a lawyer, a schoolteacher, an office worker, and others take turns leading the services.

When I preached a revival there, I asked if they planned to

call a pastor. "We want to," they replied. "We need one to train us, but we don't want a pastor who will not let us work and lead services in our homes. He won't have to do regular visitation; we do that. He could just train us and help us work with difficult individuals and situations. We haven't found a pastor yet that we thought would let us do that." I can testify that this young church does witness and does minister, for by the close of the week seventy-eight persons had accepted Christ as Savior.

One church leader has moved to the island of Sumatra to teach school. Naturally, he has begun services in several surrounding villages. Another member has helped administer disaster relief funds on an island several hundred miles from Jakarta. A third member has helped lead the associational Baptist Women's group to send a home missionary to a transmigration area in Lampung, Sumatra. Extending the kingdom has become a life-style for these Christians.

NOTES
1. Howard A. Snyder, *The Problem of the Wine Skins* (Downers Grove, Ill.: InterVarsity Press, 1976), p. 102. Used by permission.
2. Arnold B. Come, *Agents of Reconciliation* (Philadelphia: The Westminster Press, 1960), pp. 88-89. Used by permission.
3. Joseph H. Thayer, *A Greek-English Lexicon of the New Testament* (Nashville: Broadman Press, Copyright 1977 by Baker Book House; reprint of fourth edition printed in 1889), p. 321.
4. Findley B. Edge, *The Greening of the Church* (Waco: Word Books, 1971), p. 38.
5. Come, *op. cit.*, p. 94.
6. Elaine Selcraig Furlow, *The Human Touch* (Atlanta: Home Mission Board, Southern Baptist Convention, 1975), pp. 137-52.
7. *Arkansas Baptist*, Vol. 78, No. 19, May 17, 1979, p. 11.
8. *MARC Newsletter* (May 1979), p. 4.

BIBLIOGRAPHY
God's Bold Plan for Missions. Equipping Center module. Nashville: The Sunday School Board of the Southern Baptist Convention, 1979.
Grimes, Lewis Howard. *The Rebirth of the Laity.* Nashville: Abingdon Press, 1962.
Hoekendijk, Johannes Christian. *The Church Inside Out.* Philadelphia: The Westminster Press, 1966.
Manson, T. W. *The Church's Ministry.* London: Hodder & Stoughton, Ltd., 1948.
———. *Ministry and Priesthood: Christ's and Ours.* London: Epworth Press, 1958.
Trueblood, David Elton. *Your Other Vocation.* New York: Harper & Row, Publishers, Inc., 1952.

CHAPTER 9

God's Go-between

"God shapes the world by prayer. The more praying there is in the world, the better the world will be, the mightier the forces against evil. . . . The prayers of God's saints are the capital stock in heaven by which God carries on His great work upon earth. . . . God conditions the very life and prosperity of His cause on prayer."[1]

My biblical image of the spiritual warfare between the kingdom of God and the kingdom of Satan was rather weak until I visited Corinth and began to understand 2 Corinthians 10:3-5. Our family returned for our first furlough by way of Greece. We were disappointed with the old city of Corinth, because all that remains is a pile of rubble and a few pillars.

Undaunted, we drove our car to a huge, ancient fortress atop the mountain that overshadows the city. A wall wide enough for a chariot to drive on encircled the mountain. We hiked up the mountain and through the first gate, only to encounter a second wall about one hundred yards farther up the mountain. Beyond it was a third wall. My wife and daughters stopped to rest at the third gate, while my sons and I climbed to the top of the mountain. When we looked back, they appeared to be about an inch high, and we were all still inside the fortress!

I turned to look in the other direction and caught my breath at the panoramic view of the Mediterranean Sea. To the east I could see Athens. If I could have seen far enough to the west, I would have seen Rome.

Obviously, whoever controlled this fortress had authority over this part of the world. The fortress, built before the time of Paul, was not conquered until thirteen hundred years after his death.

PERSONAL LEARNING ACTIVITY 43
Read 2 Corinthians 10:3-5 and note the words that could refer symbolically to this fortress.

Paul mentioned war, weapons, strongholds, casting down high things, and bringing into captivity. He told the Corinthian Christians that they battled a spiritual enemy who was humanly invincible and that they must fight with spiritual weapons because the battle took place in the spirit world. Note that Paul's instructions dealt with the mental and the spiritual. They were to cast down *imaginations*, high things that exalted themselves against the *knowledge* of God, and to make every *thought* obedient to Christ.

We fight an enemy whose strength and cunning are surpassed only by God's strength and wisdom. We are at war! Therefore, Christ has given us spiritual weapons with which to fight. Prayer is included in the list of weapons in the spiritual warfare with the forces of Satan.

PURPOSE OF PRAYER IN MISSIONS

Our battle is not with flesh and blood but with principalities, with powers, with rulers of darkness of this world, and with spiritual wickedness in high places (Eph. 6:12). Christ already has defeated the principalities and powers through the incarnation, the crucifixion, and the resurrection. He has triumphed over them and has made a public spectacle of them (Col. 2:15). He has been raised to the throne of heaven far above all principalities, and powers, and might, and dominion (Eph. 1:20-21).

However, the battle is not finished for his body, the church. The church is to make actual the victory Christ won. God has revealed the mystery that had been hidden from the beginning of time—that all nations are to be a part of Christ's body. He called Paul and the rest of us "least saints" to preach the unsearchable riches of Christ.

PERSONAL LEARNING ACTIVITY 44
Read Ephesians 3:3-14 and write the cause you think Paul referred to when he said, "For this cause I bow my knees . . . ."

God's eternal purpose, which he purposed in Christ Jesus our Lord, is that the church should make known the manifold wisdom of God to "the principalities and powers in heavenly places" (Eph. 3:10). Paul immediately followed this statement with a statement about the boldness and access that we have to God through Christ (Eph. 3:12). He added, "For **this** cause I bow my knees unto the Father of our Lord Jesus Christ" (Eph. 3:14). Prayer is the mighty means by which the church is empowered to demonstrate the wisdom and power of God to Satan and his hierarchy of rulers and demons.

Paul E. Billheimer goes so far as to say:

. . . prayer is not primarily God's way of getting things done. It is God's way of giving the Church "on-the-job" training in overcoming the forces hostile to God. This world is a laboratory in which those who are destined for the throne are learning, by actual practice in the prayer closet, how to overcome Satan and his hierachy.[2]

PATTERN OF INTERCESSORY PRAYER

Jehoshaphat fasted and prayed when attacked by the kings of Ammon, Moab, and Mount Seir (2 Chron. 20:1-25). The whole nation prayed until God assured them that "the battle is not yours, but God's. . . . Ye shall not need to fight in this battle: set yourselves, stand ye still, and see the salvation of the Lord with you" (2 Chron. 20:15-17). They praised God for the victory; and by the time they reached the battlefield, God already had caused the three enemy armies to annihilate one another. Israel just picked up the spoils. Here is the secret of victory—win the battle in prayer first!

Daniel fasted and prayed three weeks before God answered his prayer. Daniel described the spiritual battle that was taking place in the spirit world with the words of the angel to him:

> "Don't be frightened, Daniel, for your request has been heard in heaven and was answered the very first day you began to fast before the Lord and pray for understanding; that very day I was sent here to meet you. But for twenty-one days the mighty Evil Spirit who overrules the kingdom of Persia blocked my way. Then Michael, one of the top officers of the heavenly army, came to help me, so that I was able to break through the spirit rulers of Persia. When I leave, I will go again to fight my way back, past the prince of Persia; and after him, the prince of Greece. Only Michael, the angel who guards your people Israel, will be there to help me" (Dan. 10:12-13,20-21, TLB).

The purpose of intercessory prayer in missions is to overcome the spiritual powers that rule the nations and the hearts of unsaved men. God responds to prayer and receives the glory for the victory. He uses his people as intercessors to train them in his purpose, to direct them in his battles, and to display to the evil powers his glorious plan of eternal partnership with man.

O. J. Frazier, missionary to China, literally brought thirty thousand Lisu people to Christ through prayer. His first six years in the area resulted in very little fruit among the primitive tribes. Then he began to intercede for them and to enlist prayer partners in England. God honored their spiritual warfare over the evil forces possessing the Lisu people. Once response came, Frazier noticed that the churches that he did not visit as often grew faster than those where he worked regularly. His conclusion was that he prayed more for the churches that he could not visit and, therefore, they prospered more.[3]

POWER OF PRAYING ACCORDING TO GOD'S WILL

Prayer is designed to involve us in God's purpose more than to involve God in our plans. Once we understand the purpose of God in the world, we should invest our lives in it. God delights in answering prayer that is according to his will. He refuses to answer prayer that is not in his will. Our task, then, is to discover what God wants and to ask for it.

God clearly presents his purpose and will in his Word. To pray successfully we must know his Word and base our prayers on its promises.

PERSONAL LEARNING ACTIVITY 45
Read 1 John 5:14-15. Write in your own words what it means.

We know we are praying according to his will if his Spirit reveals it in the Word. Once we have that assurance, we are confident that what we ask for has been granted. We accept it as an accomplished fact even though we must wait for the physical evidence.

The Spirit comes to guide us into all truth (John 16:13). When we pray according to truth, the Spirit intercedes for us according to the will of God (Rom. 8:27).

PERSONAL LEARNING ACTIVITY 46
Jesus' prayer reveals God's concern for us and the world. Read John 17 and make two lists: (1) what Jesus prayed for his disciples; (2) what Jesus said about the world.

When we pray for the things for which Jesus prayed, we know we pray in God's will. He prayed for his disciples more than he prayed for the world, because he was sending them to the world. Just so, our focus also should be on Christ's disciples and their ministry to the world.

God decided long ago that he would not save the world apart from his people. His concern for the world is linked to the concern his people have. He did not tell us to send out laborers into the harvest. He said, "The harvest truly is plenteous, but the labourers are few; pray ye therefore the Lord of the harvest, that he will send forth labourers into his harvest" (Matt. 9:37-38).

The reason we have so few people reaping the harvest is because we are not praying that the Lord will send out laborers. As I write this book, I am praying that the Lord will impress and send you, along with a spiritual army of laborers, into the ripe harvest fields of the world. He sends each of us into the nearby harvest fields in our communities. He sends many of us to other nations.

Jesus prays that the Father will keep us from evil (or "the Evil One" [John 17:15, GNB]). He engaged in spiritual warfare for us and is now interceding for us at the right hand of God.

PERSONAL LEARNING ACTIVITY 47
Read the following verses and write the most outstanding common quality of these men of prayer: Genesis 16:8-13; 18:16-33; Exodus 32:7-14; Numbers 14:11-21; and Isaiah 62:1-9.

The intercessors you have just read about prevailed in prayer; God spared his people and continued his purpose through them. But when there were no intercessors, God did not spare the people. "I sought for a man among them, that should make up the hedge, and stand in the gap before me for the land, that I should not destroy it: but I found none" (Ezek. 22:30).

The biographies of George Meuller, Praying Hyde, Hudson Taylor, Rees Howells, and other great intercessors reveal a common pattern. They sought God's will about a matter until the Spirit impressed them with a Scripture. Then they claimed the Scripture promise by faith, and God answered their prayers.

Examine your prayer list and prayer life to see if you are praying according to God's purpose. Are you praying for the world? Are you engaged in spiritual warfare? Are you praying for laborers for the harvest?

POSITION OF THE INTERCESSOR

New Testament priests are to intercede for others. Each Christian bears the responsibility to come to God first for his own sins and, second, for the sins of others. Paul wrote, "I exhort therefore, that, first of all, supplications, prayers, intercessions, and giving of thanks, be made for all men . . . for this is good and acceptable in the sight of God our Saviour; who will have all men to be saved, and to come unto the knowledge of the truth" (1 Tim. 2:1-4).

The position of the intercessor is directly between God and the one for whom prayer is made. The Old Testament priest illustrated this when he came before the mercy seat to intercede for the people. Jesus took the position of the intercessor in Gethsemane and on the cross. When he died, the veil to the holy of holies was split from top to bottom, symbolizing the access that all believers have to the Father through Christ. Jesus presently sits at the right hand of the Father and intercedes for us. This is one reason we pray in Jesus' name.

Moses placed himself in the position of the Israelites when he prayed: "Oh, this people have sinned a great sin, and have made them gods of gold. Yet now, if thou wilt forgive their sin—; and if not, blot me, I pray thee, out of thy book which thou hast written" (Ex. 32:31-32). He was willing to take their punishment, even to being blotted out of God's book.

Paul said: "I have great heaviness and continual sorrow in my heart. For I could wish that myself were accursed from Christ for my brethren, my kinsmen according to the flesh" (Rom. 9:2-3). Paul positioned himself between God and his people with an urgency that caused him to be willing to go to hell in their place. He could plead with men for God because he had pleaded so fervently with God for men.

Rees Howells so identified with those for whom he prayed that he often felt compelled to identify with their physical conditions. As he prayed for tramps, he felt he should eat what they could get at the British government's lodging houses. So for two and one-half years he ate only two meals—of bread, cheese, and soup—a day. God greatly used him in ministering to the indigent.

After interceding for four orphans, Howells felt led to take them into his home. He prayed intensely for God to give him a father's love. He was then able to say:

"Any child without parents has a claim on God to be a Father to him, so these four orphans had a claim on the Holy Spirit who was to be a Father to them through me. . . . I felt I loved every little child in the world that had no one to look after it. It was the love of God flowing through me.". . . That is the law of intercession on every level of life, that only so far as we have been tested and proved willing to do a thing ourselves, can we intercede for others.[4]

Howells' intercession prepared him for missionary service in Africa. God sent great revival there in answer to his prayers. Later Howells gave himself full time to intercession. According to Norman Grubb, Howells' biographer, battles of World War II were won because of his prayers and those of his prayer partners. Howells' final intercessory prayer victory was for the Lord to provide one hundred thouand pounds for the spreading of the gospel to every person.

Where among Baptists are the intercessors who will give their lives in the spiritual warfare of prayer for the world? When will every believer realize his priesthood and spend part of his time in intercession for missions? We should position ourselves between God and those who need him so desperately.

PLAN FOR INTERCESSION

Because we wrestle not with flesh and blood, God provides spiritual armor for the intercessor. We must realize that we are behind enemy lines and that spiritual warfare goes on all around us. Our natural inclination is to fight with physical means.

How does one fight a spiritual warfare in prayer? Ephesians 6:10-20 lists the spiritual armor for prayer warfare: "Praying always with all prayer and supplication in the Spirit, and watching thereunto with all perseverance and supplication for all saints" (Eph. 6:18). Each piece of this armor is essential to the prayer warrior.

One of the most important days of my life I awoke feeling terribly depressed. This was unusual for me. Then I realized I was not really depressed but oppressed. I had no idea of the importance of the day, but obviously Satan did. As soon as I recognized this oppressive spirit, I knelt by the bed and used the prayer armor of Ephesians 6 to gain the victory. It was a great day, and God won the victory in some very important decisions.

The enemy is defined in Ephesians 6:11-12 as various levels of evil spiritual rulers. Satan uses his tricks to defeat the saints even in prayer (v. 11). Most Christians think they are immune to Satan's attack when they are on their knees, but that is precisely when Satan is most active. He hates to see even the weakest saint on his knees.

God wants us to *stand against* (v. 11) Satan with all his wiles in spiritual warfare. He wants us to *withstand* (v. 13) in the evil day and then finally to conquer and to be *standing* when the battle is over (v. 13).

The prayer armor should be used specifically in the following situations. First, when Satan attacks us. Second, when we attack Satan and enter his realm to claim those he has captured—the strayed and the lost. Third, when we are seeking release from Satan's dominion over some area of our own lives. Satan jealously guards all that he has captured and will surrender it only when forced to by God.

Look at each part of the armor and relate it to prayer. The *helmet of salvation* may symbolize protection of the mind, a favorite place for Satan to begin. Satan places doubt, disobedience, and dread in the mind (2 Cor. 10:5). When you begin praying, place the helmet of salvation securely on your head by claiming the blood of Christ as the basis of your right to pray (Rev. 12:11), by praising God for your salvation and your assurance (Ps. 145), by giving thanks to God for your salvation and all its attendant blessings (Eph. 5:19-20), and by claiming the mind of Christ (Rom. 8:5).

The *breastplate of righteousness* may symbolize protection for the heart. All evil comes out of the heart (Mark 7:20-23). At this point, ask the Lord to search your heart and show you any wicked way in it (Ps. 139:23-24). As the Spirit reveals sin in your heart, confess it (1 John 1:9) and claim Christ's righteousness as the substitute for it (2 Cor. 5:21). After you have confessed your sins and have claimed Christ's righteousness, picture the breastplate of righteousness securely fastened so that Satan cannot get to your heart.

The loincloth, or the *belt of truth,* may represent the protection of the emotions (usually thought to reside in the solar plexus). Determine to want nothing but truth and integrity in your life and prayer. Examine your evaluation of things, words, and feelings, and then surrender all of them to God in exchange for truth. This makes you more objective in your praying and in your living and less vulnerable to Satan's lies. Ask God not to allow your emotions to cloud the truth. The belt held all the armor of the Roman soldiers in place; truth makes our spiritual armor secure.

Having your *feet shod with the preparation of the gospel of peace* puts you in a position to attack the enemy (Isa. 52:7-8). This means you are prepared to take the gospel to anyone for whom you pray. If you are not ready to take the gospel, it will be difficult for you to intercede for lost persons. Envision the countries of the world where the gospel needs to be taken and pray for them as well as for your friends and your neighbors.

The *shield of faith* fends off Satan's attacks as you advance. He tries to shoot his fiery darts through your mind, heart, and emotions, but God gives you the shield of faith to ward them off. The faith shield is used for advance, not retreat. With this shield you overcome the world (1 John 5:4). Neither temptations nor trials can pierce the shield of faith. Faith is the key to winning the victory in prayer. Jesus told his disciples, "What things soever ye desire, when ye pray, believe that ye receive them, and ye shall have them" (Mark 11:24).

The *sword of the Spirit* is the Word of God. Spiritual victory cannot be attained apart from the Word. The shield of faith is most effective with the sword of the Spirit. As you march into Satan's territory and begin to reclaim for God the things that Satan has stolen out of his kingdom, ask for those things which

God reveals through his Word. Find Bible promises and use them to claim that which God really wants to give you. Satan cannot withstand the Word of God and falls back when you move in to possess God's possessions through claiming his Word by faith.

The armor prepares you to intercede for others. Now you are in position to pray for others and to expect an answer. The battle is on! Advance clothed with the armor of God. Persevere in intercession until the victory is won and you stand victorious with your trophies of grace. Intercession pleads that God's plan be executed and that his gospel be proclaimed boldly (Eph. 6:19-20).

PERSONAL LEARNING ACTIVITY 48
List each part of the armor. Write one sentence about each, describing its function in preparing you for intecessory prayer.

You cannot pray like this in five minutes. Spiritual warfare means wrestling with the enemy. It may take an hour, or a day, or a week, or longer. God is looking for soldiers armed for combat. In fact, he has limited himself to prayer warriors. Every advance of the kingdom is dependent on the prayers of the saints. God is determined that we should be full partners in claiming the kingdom and, therefore, waits until we have put on the prayer armor and entered the spiritual warfare.

Each Christian should set aside special times for prayer warfare in addition to his regular times of prayer. It may begin with an hour a week and then be stretched to a day of fasting and prayer. The job of a prayer warrior is not for retired saints only. God intends for all of us to be praying always with all prayers and supplications. The greatest privilege he gives us is the privilege of fighting in his army on behalf of those who have been captured by the Evil One.

PRIORITY OF INTERCESSORY PRAYER IN MISSIONS

John Wesley said, "God will do nothing but in answer to prayer." All advances in the kingdom are preceded by prayer. No revival ever begins without prayer. When God wants to do something, he moves men to pray for it. Trace the movements of God in history, and you will find they were born in prayer, bathed in prayer, and grew by prayer.

PERSONAL LEARNING ACTIVITY 49
Read the following passages and cite the movement that was born in prayer: Exodus 3:1-10; Nehemiah 1:4-10; Matthew 4:1-11; Acts 1:12 to 2:47; and Acts 13:1-13.

The birthplace of the American foreign missionary movement was a prayer meeting in a haystack near Williamstown, Massachusetts, in 1806. A spiritual awakening in the churches motivated Samuel John Mills and four friends to pray outdoors twice a week. One Saturday afternoon they ran to a large haystack for protection from a thunderstorm. They prayed and talked about Asia, which they had studied in class. Mills declared that they must send the gospel to the heathen. One disagreed, saying that civilization must precede Christianity. They knelt to pray to be united in purpose. As they finished praying Mills cried out, "We can do it, if we will." Later in Andover Theological Seminary, Adoniram Judson joined Mills's prayer group and became the first missionary of the American Board for Foreign Missions.

God's mission to the world begins when his people get on their knees.

Importunity gives God an opportunity to demonstrate his power. Intercessory prayer is not to be done at our convenience but because of someone's inconvenience. Jesus said, "Ask . . . seek . . . knock" (Matt. 7:7). We must make priority what God makes priority.

When God led us to the mission field, he laid on my heart the need for intercessors. I realized that I was a very ordinary person, and I said, "God, I would like to see what you can do with an average person who is backed by prayer." Through the years several thousand people have prayed for us, some without missing a day. Each month in our prayer letter I asked them to pray about specific needs. In the weeks and months that followed, I reported on how God had accomplished his work through their prayers. Literally hundreds of answers to prayer have been recorded as a direct result of intercessory prayer by people in the United States. If every missionary had people praying daily for his specific requests, a great surge of power would be felt all over the world.

PRACTICE OF PRAYER FOR MISSIONS

Every local church should have an intercessory prayer ministry enveloping local, associational, state, national, and international missions. We must develop trifocal vision which allows us to pray for the needs near at home, the needs in our nation, the needs around the world. Prayer is the one ministry that supports all of the other ministries of the church. Our failure to accomplish God's will is not so much for lack of strategy or of activities as for the lack of prayer. Most churches have programs for everything except prayer.

Individuals should have a systematic, daily prayer ministry for others. In your prayer ministry, each day you might pray for a different area of the world, or for different types of ministries, or for different persons on mission.

The Woman's Missionary Union provides guidance in prayer for home and foreign missionaries. The Week of Prayer for Home Missions and the Week of Prayer for Foreign Missions, as well as state weeks of prayer for state and associational missions, should be on everyone's agenda. Periodicals, such as *World Mission Journal, Royal Service, Home Missions, The Commission, Contempo,* and *Baptist Adults* in Church Training, provide up-to-date requests and missionary birthdays. No Baptist need say he is uninformed about prayer needs. But information without application is deadening.

Twenty years after I had been converted in a little rescue mission in Fort Worth, Texas, I returned to preach. Mrs. Ferguson still directed the services. She was so thrilled that one who had been saved in the mission had returned to preach. Before the service began she gathered all the derelicts around to sing "Amazing Grace." Her hands, gnarled by arthritis, sought the notes on the ancient, upright piano.

After the song she gathered everyone around for prayer. She said in a voice that broke, "Come on, men, we are going to pray for a **worldwide revival!**"

I was astonished at the fervor with which she prayed for the Spirit to be poured out on the nations of the world. She is dead now, but her cracked voice intermingled with sobs for a lost world still rings in my heart, "Brother Willis, we must pray for a worldwide revival!"

I have continued to pray for God to answer that prayer. Will you join the growing band of people around the world who will pray for the desire of God's heart to become reality, for the Spirit to be poured out, and for the gospel to be preached to every person? God waits for intercessors to be his go-betweens.

NOTES
1. E. M. Bounds, *Purpose in Prayer* (Chicago: Moody Press, n.d.), pp. 9-10. Used by permission.
2. Paul E. Billheimer, *Destined for the Throne* (Fort Washington, Pa.: Christian Literature Crusade, Inc., 1975), p. 40.
3. Mrs. Howard Taylor, *Behind the Ranges* (Chicago: Moody Press, 1964).
4. Norman P. Grubb, *Rees Howells, Intercessor* (Fort Washington, Pa.: Christian Literature Crusade, Inc., 1976). pp. 97-98.

BIBLIOGRAPHY
How to Pray for Others. Equipping Center module. The Sunday School Board of the Southern Baptist Convention, 1979.

CHAPTER 10

Mission Accomplished

An eleven-year-old boy, engrossed in an adventure book, protested when told to go to bed. He pleaded to no avail that he must find out whether the hero would escape from an impossible situation and would rescue the heroine from the clutches of the villain. Later, with the aid of a flashlight beneath the bedcovers, he read the final chapter of the book. Sure enough, the hero rescued the heroine, and the villain was captured and was put in jail. However, because he could not imagine how such a turnabout had happened, he began reading again at the place he had been forced to stop. Each time the villain did something wrong the boy said, "If you knew what I know, you wouldn't be acting like you are."

If we really believed what God has told us about how his story ends, we would live differently.

Christians have an edge on the rest of the world—God has shared the future with us. We know the secret—no matter how dark the situation may appear—God's kingdom will triumph!

Recall the situation described in chapter 1. God intended to involve man in a partnership to establish his kingdom. Satan opposed God's authority, seduced man, and enslaved him in the kingdom of evil. Each chapter of this book has revealed the increasing intensity of that conflict.

You already have pledged your allegiance to Jesus as Lord. The time has come for you to pray for the kingdom's coming, to be aware of its presence, and to be committed to its full realization.

Jesus came announcing the kingdom and calling on men to repent. He summed up his mission and God's intention in that one phrase—the kingdom of God. The kingdom arrived when the King appeared. The kingdom began to reign in men's hearts as they accepted the King. It continues to spread each time someone believes the gospel. It will culminate with every knee bowing and every tongue confessing that Jesus Christ is Lord.

God alone establishes his kingdom. He has done his part up to now and is ready to finish the job. However, he is giving us every chance to become partners with him in establishing the kingdom. He wants us to reign with him someday. The time of Christ's coming and complete victory has been hidden from us so we will be about our Father's business always. We have had the gospel revealed to us so that we can reveal it to the world before judgment day.

PERSONAL LEARNING ACTIVITY 51
1. **Read in Matthew 13 the seven parables of the kingdom. Write a sentence or two about each, explaining why it is imperative for us to put Christ's kingdom first.**
2. **Read Matthew 21:33-43 to discover what will happen if we do not fulfill God's intention.**

Throughout this book we have watched God on mission establishing his kingdom and working his plan to redeem and to restore that which man lost and Satan corrupted. Now I want you to glimpse and to feel a little of what God's triumph will be like. Pause and pray that God will open your understanding as you reverently read God's revelation of his mission being accomplished. Read the following passages for the overall impact rather than specific details. We need the same inspiration and sense of ultimate victory that the first-century Christians who received John's letter needed.

"I looked, and lo, in heaven an open door! And the first voice, which I had heard speaking to me like a trumpet, said, 'Come up hither, and I will show you what must take place after this' " (Rev. 4:1, RSV).

"I saw a Lamb standing, as though it had been slain. And when he had taken the scroll, the four living creatures and the twenty-four elders fell down before the Lamb . . . and they sang

a new song, saying, 'Worthy art thou to take the scroll and to open its seals, for thou wast slain and by thy blood didst ransom men for God from every tribe and tongue and people and nation, and hast made them a kingdom and priests to our God, and they shall reign on the earth.' Then I looked, and I heard around the throne and the living creatures and the elders the voice of many angels, numbering myriads of myriads and thousands of thousands, saying with a loud voice, 'Worthy is the Lamb who was slain, to receive power and wealth and wisdom and might and honor and glory and blessing!' And I heard every creature in heaven and on earth and under the earth and in the sea, and all therein, saying, 'To him who sits upon the throne and to the Lamb be blessing and honor and glory and might for ever and ever!' And the four living creatures said, 'Amen!' and the elders fell down and worshiped'' (Rev. 5:6,8-14, RSV).

"After this I looked, and behold, a great multitude which no man could number, from every nation, from all tribes and peoples and tongues, standing before the throne and before the Lamb, clothed in white robes, with palm branches in their hands, and crying out with a loud voice, 'Salvation belongs to our God who sits upon the throne, and to the Lamb!' And all the angels stood round the throne and round the elders and the four living creatures, and they fell on their faces before the throne and worshiped God, saying, 'Amen! Blessing and glory and wisdom and thanksgiving and honor and power and might be to God for ever and ever! Amen' '' (Rev. 7:9-12, RSV).

"Then the seventh angel blew his trumpet, and there were loud voices in heaven, saying, 'The kingdom of the world has become the kingdom of our Lord and of his Christ, and he shall reign for ever and ever' '' (Rev. 11:15, RSV).

"The great dragon was thrown down, that ancient serpent, who is called the Devil and Satan, the deceiver of the whole world—he was thrown down to the earth, and his angels were thrown down with him. And I heard a loud voice in heaven saying, 'Now the salvation and the power and the kingdom of our God and the authority of his Christ have come, for the accuser of our brethren has been thrown down, who accuses them day and night before our God. And they have conquered him by the blood of the Lamb and by the word of their testimony, for they loved not their lives even unto death. Rejoice then, O heaven and you that dwell therein! But woe to you, O earth and sea, for the devil has come down to you in great wrath, because he knows that his time is short!' " (Rev. 12:9-12, RSV).

"The devil who had deceived them was thrown into the lake of fire and sulphur where the beast and the false prophet were, and they will be tormented day and night for ever and ever. Then Death and Hades were thrown into the lake of fire. This is the second death, the lake of fire; and if any one's name was not found written in the book of life, he was thrown into the lake of fire" (Rev. 20:10,14-15, RSV).

"Then I saw a new heaven and a new earth; for the first heaven and the first earth had passed away, and the sea was no more. And I saw the holy city, new Jerusalem, coming down out of heaven from God, prepared as a bride adorned for her husband; and I heard a loud voice from the throne saying, 'Behold, the dwelling of God is with men. He will dwell with them, and they shall be his people, and God himself will be with them; he will wipe away every tear from their eyes, and death shall be no more, neither shall there be mourning nor crying nor pain any more, for the former things have passed away.' And he who sat upon the throne said, 'Behold, I make all things new' " (Rev. 21:1-5, RSV).

"And I saw no temple in the city, for its temple is the Lord God the Almighty and the Lamb. And the city has no need of sun or moon to shine upon it, for the glory of God is its light, and its lamp is the Lamb. By its light shall the nations walk; and the kings of the earth shall bring their glory into it, and its gates shall never be shut by day—and there shall be no night there; they shall bring into it the glory and the honor of the nations. But nothing unclean shall enter it, nor any one who practices abomination or falsehood, but only those who are written in the Lamb's book of life" (Rev. 21:22-27, RSV).

"Then he showed me the river of the water of life, bright as crystal, flowing from the throne of God and of the Lamb through *the middle of the street of the city; also, on either side of the river, the tree of life with its twelve kinds of fruit, yielding its fruit each month; and the leaves of the tree were for the healing of the nations. There shall no more be anything accursed, but the throne of God and of the Lamb shall be in it, and his servants shall worship him; they shall see his face, and his name shall be on their foreheads. And night shall be no more; they need no light of lamp or sun, for the Lord God will be their light, and they shall reign for ever and ever" (Rev. 22:1-5, RSV).*

" 'I Jesus have sent my angel to you with this testimony for the churches. I am the root and the offspring of David, the bright morning star.' The Spirit and the Bride say, 'Come.' And let him who hears say, 'Come.' And let him who is thirsty come, let him who desires take the water of life without price. . . . He who testifies to these things says, 'Surely I am coming soon.' Amen. Come, Lord Jesus!" (Rev. 22:16-17,20, RSV).

PERSONAL LEARNING ACTIVITY 52
Meditate on the preceding selected verses and then write in your own words the feelings you have about God's mission accomplished.

God revealed the end-time events to John so his people could catch a vision of the glorious triumph. First-century Christians struggling with their trials and their temptations had begun to lose sight of the kingdom picture. Many modern Christians surrounded by affluence and mired in complacency have lost their vision of the kingdom also.

Contrast that with the eager disciples who asked, "Lord, wilt thou at this time restore again the kingdom to Israel?" (Acts 1:6). Jesus had to tell them not to bother about how soon the kingdom would come but to witness to all men. The zeal of their witness revealed the impact of God's impending victory.

In Ephesians 1:9-10 God reveals that in the "dispensation of the fulness of times" he will gather together all things in Christ.

The word translated *dispensation* means *stewardship*. God is saying that as a steward ordered and managed a household in that day so he is ordering all things to bring together everything in Christ. Only a part of the hundreds of promises telling of the glory, the majesty, and the triumph of the kingdom have been fulfilled. God commands us to prepare for their complete fulfillment in Christ's second coming.

God will establish the kingdom, but he has given us a strategic role to play in the realization of it. Paul used the same word, dispensation or stewardship, in describing his responsibility in the world. "I am made a minister, according to the *dispensation* of God which is given to me for you, to fulfil the word of God . . . which is Christ in you, the hope of glory: whom we preach, warning *every* man, and teaching *every* man in all wisdom; that we may present *every* man perfect in Christ Jesus: whereunto I also labour, striving according to his working, which worketh in me mightily" (Col. 1:25-29). Paul felt he had been given a responsibility to preach, to teach, and to present every man perfect in Christ. We have the same stewardship.

Plainly, the New Testament teaches that the kingdom of God has come in Christ and even now is in the world, but it is also yet to come. How are we to live in this kingdom that has come but has not yet come, is victorious yet waiting for the victory?

We must live as the early church lived—with the eager expectancy of the imminent end and the confident assurance that only God can establish the kingdom. We must obey Christ's commission and demonstrate our faith in that kingdom unto death. We must decide to seek the kingdom of God first and to live only for his will to be done, on earth as it is in heaven. Our witnessing and our preaching must capture again the intense urgency of the New Testament because the time is short and the last days have come.

Our generation is living in the "last days." They began at Pentecost and will end with all the kingdoms of the world being offered up to God by Christ. Three Jewish feasts symbolized the fulfillment of God's eternal plan. At the Feast of the Passover Christ became the sacrificial lamb for the sins of the world. At the Feast of Pentecost the Holy Spirit reaped the firstfruits of Christ's victory over death. At a future time, symbolized by the Feast of the Tabernacles, there will be a celebration of the full harvest—the marriage feast of the Lamb. We live in the parentheses between the coming of the Holy Spirit and the second coming of Jesus Christ and are charged with the reaping of the harvest.

Our urgency relates both to the impending judgment of God on man's sin and the promise that God will deal in mercy with those who believe in him. We have only two alternatives to our kingdom tension: (1) give up all hope and responsibility for this world, retire from it, and let it go its suicidal way to hell; or (2) by aggressive witness, fulfill our stewardship in God's establishing of the kingdom.

> "If the redemption of man awaits his faith in Christ and his Kingdom, then to summon men to that faith is no fussy meddling; it is the pivotal activity of history. . . . The redemption of man awaits precisely the birth of a new and redeemed race of men. And the Kingdom of God is that new race of men, God's living Church. In her is that ever-coming Kingdom."[1]

We are a generation of priests chosen to reign with the King. If we are to reign with Christ in the coming kingdom, we must serve during its rise to power.

PERSONAL LEARNING ACTIVITY 53
Read the following verses about our reigning with Christ: Luke 22:29-30; Revelation 1:6; 3:21; 5:10; 20:6; Hebrews 12:28-29. After reading these verses make a list of the things that you feel you should be doing during the remaining time God has alloted you on earth.

As soon as possible, we must take the gospel to every person, disciple those who follow Christ, and establish reproducing churches among every people in the world.

THE WILL OF GOD

We must evangelize the world because God wills it. The Lord is
"not willing that any should perish, but that all should
come to repentance. But the day of the Lord will come
as a thief in the night; in which the heavens shall pass
away with a great noise, and the elements shall melt
with fervent heat, the earth also and the works therein
shall be burned up. Seeing then that all these things
shall be dissolved, what manner of persons are ye to be
in all holy conversation and godliness, looking for and
hastening unto the coming of the day of God" (2 Pet.
3:9-12).

Every action of God has shown that he wants a people who
will do his will on earth as it is done in heaven. Christ died for it
to be accomplished. The Holy Spirit works day and night to
convict men of sin and to inspire Christians to carry the message
of salvation to them.

NEEDS OF THE WORLD

Need, like a gaping sore, infects the entire human race. Crawl
inside the skin of over a billion people who will go to bed tonight
hungry. Feel the pain of disease-ravaged bodies. Touch the
sightless eyes. Listen to the silence of deafness. Walk through
this world of need, and you will be crushed by your total inability
to meet a fraction of it. Feel the turmoil of broken homes, the
loss of murdered loved ones, the emptiness of a world without
hope.

Yet, all these are but symptoms of man's greatest
problem—lostness. Matthew 6:23 says, "If therefore the light
that is in thee be darkness, how great is that darkness!" How can
light be darkness? Every man has received some light from God,
but he has distorted and misused it to his own damnation. Every
religion is an example of men's taking a truth and so overem-
phasizing it as to blind themselves to God's full truth. Moslems
so overemphasize the transcendency and omnipotence of God

that they cannot believe that God in Christ could or would come to die for them. Hindus emphasize the omnipresence of God to the extent of believing there are millions of manifestations of God, yet they are scandalized by the news that Jesus is the only way of salvation. Buddhists so emphasize the evil world that they cannot believe that Christ would be made sin for us. So, if the light that they have is made darkness, how great is that darkness! Their only hope is in the Light of the world seen by the single eye.

UNCERTAINTY OF THE FUTURE

The uncertainty of the future of this world demands urgency in proclaiming the kingdom. The impending wrath of God on all unrighteousness has been withheld only because of God's longsuffering toward man. "God is angry with the wicked every day" (Ps. 7:11). They treasure up "wrath against the day of wrath and revelation of the righteous judgment of God" (Rom. 2:5). Men must be warned that in the future they shall cry to the mountains and rocks to "fall on us, and hide us from the face of him that sitteth on the throne, and from the wrath of the Lamb: for the great day of his wrath has come; and who shall be able to stand?" (Rev. 6:16-17).

God warns us that "the time is come that judgment must begin at the house of God: and if it first begin at us, what shall the end be of them that obey not the gospel of God?" (1 Pet. 4:17). America as a nation and the church as God's people stand under his judgment. Only because of his mercy we are not already consumed. A comparison of our nation with Romans 1:18-32 should convince anyone that we are living under the as yet unleashed wrath of God.

On the other hand, the world seems bent on destroying itself. The threat of a nuclear holocaust, shortages of oil and food, and the burgeoning selfishness of men and nations gives an omen of disaster. The "have not" nations are demanding their right to share the abundance of the "haves." The long mistreated former colonies may rise to demand their share of the world's goods. As starving people they have nothing to lose and may risk using nuclear weapons.

The uncertainty of the future demands that we take the gospel to every nation while there is still time.

POSSIBILITIES OF THIS AGE

The hand of God has moved in the affairs of men and of nations to produce throughout the world an unprecedented responsiveness to the gospel. Donald McGavran says: "More winnable people live in the world today than ever before. India has far more now than in the days of Carey or Clough. Africa has myriads who can be won. Latin America teems with opportunity. For the Gospel, never before has such a day of opportunity dawned. These populations have not become receptive by accident."[2]

God is not a mere spectator watching to see what men will do; he is an active participant in the redemption of lost humanity. He did not give us a command to disciple all nations only to wait to see if we would do it. He said, "I am with you always, even to the end of the age" (Matt. 28:20, NASB). God is working in the lives of his children to send them into the harvest; he also is working in the people of the world to prepare them for the witness of his people. We must see his hand in the rising of the masses to seek a better life, in the restlessness of the nations.

Oswald Smith points up this urgency with the following illustration:

In our Canadian Northwest we have great fields. Every autumn special trains loaded with harvesters are rushed to those fields. Why the haste? Why the hurry? Why not take our time? Why not do it later? Why must it be done now? Because it is now or never. The harvest will not wait. There may be another, but this harvest will be lost, and lost forever. It must be garnered within the limits of a single harvest season or it will perish. Hence the haste. So it is with the Lord's harvest. There may be those who will reach a future generation, but this generation will be lost and will perish unevangelized. Hence the urgency.[3]

As I did the research for my book *Indonesian Revival: Why Two Million Came to Christ,* I became convinced that the hand of God moves in all the affairs of men—not just his religious affairs—to create responsiveness to the gospel. It is as if God wears a glove with each successive finger inscribed with the words: culture, politics, society, economics, and religion. God's hand is moving throughout all the affairs of men and of nations to produce a harvest. God's Spirit is also working in the hearts of his people to thrust forth laborers into his already ripened harvest.

In addition to sending missionaries on career or on a short-term basis, we must establish in every country churches that grow their own leaders and are a part of their culture. The first reason is that it is impossible to send enough personnel; the second is that the majority of people will respond only when one of their own countrymen shares the gospel with them. We must build these churches to equip each member to function as part of the body of Christ.

Modern technology has expanded our reach and has shrunk the world to a reachable size. Television, radio, and other modern means of communication make it possible to sow the seed. Improved living conditions and transportation make it easier for Christians to go and to reap the harvest.

IMMINENCE OF CHRIST'S RETURN

Our hope for deliverance, the second coming of Christ, is also a motivation to take the gospel of deliverance to those who do not know him. Jesus' teaching is filled with warnings of his sudden, imminent return. He is bringing this age to a close.

Watch therefore: for ye know not what hour your Lord doth come. But know this, that if the goodman of the house had known in what watch the thief would come, he would have watched, and would not have suffered his house to be broken up. Therefore be ye also ready: for in such an hour as ye think not the Son of man cometh (Matt. 24:42-44).

CONCLUSION

Missions began in the heart of God and shapes all his dealings with the world. He revealed his purpose to his Chosen People, but they rejected their missionary calling and prostituted it on themselves by interpreting the election as their exclusive right. Nevertheless, they provided a vehicle through which God's purpose could be revealed in his Son.

Jesus fulfilled God's purpose by becoming Servant, Priest, and King. He called a people to fulfill the same role. The Holy Spirit came to inspire them, to motivate them, and to empower them to go to the uttermost parts of the earth with the good news and to establish his disciples in churches.

The church as the body of Christ inherits the role of Israel that was fulfilled by Christ. The church must serve as disciplined children, suffering servants, and ministering priests to carry out God's purpose in the world. As a pilgrim church it suffers because the world will not accept its credentials. It lives in the tension of the last days, longing for the establishment of God's kingdom. This tension began with the resurrection and Pentecost, when the new age was ushered in, and has been the church's constant companion whenever it has dared to follow its Lord in ministering to the world. The church is God's instrument in the world. It is the present embodiment of God's election purpose. It is equipped to make disciples, to build up the body, and to spread the kingdom. It kneels between a lost world and a coming Lord.

Missions is the work of the triune God. The world is the sphere of his mission. The church is the sign of God's mission in the world and is his partner in the coming kingdom. The church exists to minister and to witness to the world.

The world awaits the witness. One morning I took several seminary students to visit in an area of Semarang, Indonesia, approximately two miles from our home. Within two hours I witnessed to four women who had never heard of Jesus Christ. One of the women invited me into her humble, split-bamboo home. We sat on mats on the dirt floor because there was no furniture.

I had the thrill of telling her the good news. It was news. I told her how Christ came to a darkened world that was seeking the light. I described his crucifixion at the hands of evil men and then hastened to assure her that he had arisen from the dead three days later. She asked breathlessly, "When?" as if it had just happened.

As I tried to explain that it had happened almost two thousand years ago, I could see in her face a question forming? "If this Jesus is as important as you seem to think he is, why have I never heard about him? Why have my parents never heard about him?"

I bent my head and struggled for an answer. I looked up and said: "Lady, it is not God's fault. God has done everything necessary for all the world to be saved. He gave his only Son, and that Son died for our sins. Then he told his followers to take the gospel to every person. Forgive me for never telling you before today; forgive all of us Christians for not doing what our Lord commanded us."

In the middle of the dirt floor was a basket turned upside down over a mother hen. Little chicks jumped in and out through holes in the basket. I said: "We are a lot like the little chicks that want to get back to their mother. Jesus once said that he would like to gather us to himself as a hen gathers her chicks under her wings, but we would not come. As the chicks grow older, it will become impossible for them to get back through the holes to their mother under the basket. The basket is like our sins that separate us from God. Jesus' paying for our sins was like lifting the basket and saying, 'Come back to the Father.'"

That day the lady trusted all she knew of herself and her sin to what she knew of God and her Savior.

Millions who have never heard would come to Christ if someone would take the good news to them. God waits on us to fulfill our mission.

NOTES
1. John Bright, *The Kingdom of God* (Nashville: Abingdon Press, 1953), p. 258. Used by permission.
2. Donald A. McGavran, *Understanding Church Growth* (Grand Rapids: William

B. Eerdmans Publishing Co.; 1970), pp. 58-59. Used by permission.
3. M. A. Doroch, *How Shall They Hear?* (Grand Rapids: Zondervan Publishing Company, 1958), p. 35.

BIBLIOGRAPHY
Bright, John. *The Kingdom of God.* Nashville: Abingdon Press, 1953.
Willis, Avery T., Jr. *Indonesian Revival: Why Two Million Came to Christ.* South Pasadena, Calif.: William Carey Library, 1977.

The Church Study Course

The Church Study Course consists of a variety of short-term credit courses for adults and youth and noncredit foundational units for children and preschoolers. The materials are for use in addition to the study and training curriculums made available to the churches on an ongoing basis.

Study courses and foundational units are organized into a system that is promoted by the Sunday School Board, 127 Ninth Avenue, North, Nashville, Tennessee 37234; by the Woman's Missionary Union, 600 North Twentieth Street, Birmingham, Alabama 35203; by the Brotherhood Commission, 1548 Poplar Avenue, Memphis, Tennessee 38104; and by the respective departments of the state conventions affiliated with the Southern Baptist Convention.

Study course materials are flexible enough to be adapted to the needs of any Baptist church. The resources are published in several different formats—textbooks of various sizes, workbooks, kits, and modules. Each item contains an explanation of the Church Study Course.

Types of Study and Credit

Adults and youth can earn study course credit through individual or group study. Teachers of courses or of foundational units are eligible to receive credit.

1. *Class experience.*—Group involvement with course material for the designated number of hours for the particular course. Study course credit requirements call for a person to

158

read, view, or listen to the course material and to attend class sessions. A person who is absent from one or more sessions must complete the Personal Learning Activities or other requirements for the material missed.

2. *Individual study.*—This includes reading, viewing, or listening to course material and completing the specified requirements for the course.

3. *Lesson course study.*—Parallel use of designated study course material during the study of selected units in Church Program Organization periodical curriculum units. Guidance for credit appears in the selected periodical.

4. *Institutional study.*—Parallel use of designated study course material during regular courses at educational institutions, including Seminary Extension Department courses. Guidance for this means of credit is provided by the teacher.

Credit is awarded for the successful completion of a course of study. This credit is granted by the Church Study Course Awards Office, 127 Ninth Avenue, North, Nashville, Tennessee 37234, for the participating agencies. Credit may be requested on Form 151, Church Study Course Credit Request, Revised 1975.

When credit is issued to a person on request, the Awards Office sends two copies of a notice of credit earned to the church. The original copy of the credit slip should be filed by the study course clerk in the participant's record of training folder. The duplicate should be given to the person who earned the credit. Accumulated credits are applied toward a specific leadership diploma or the Christian Development Diplomas, which are measures of learning, growth, development, and training.

Detailed information about the Church Study Course system of credits, diplomas, and record keeping is available from the participating agencies. Study course materials, supplementary teaching or learning aids, and forms for record keeping may be ordered from Baptist Book Stores.

The Church Study Course Curriculum
Credit is granted on those courses listed in the current copy of

Church Services and Materials Catalog and Church Study Course Catalog. When selecting courses of foundational units, the current catalogs should be checked to determine what study course materials are valid.

HOW TO REQUEST CREDIT FOR THIS COURSE

This book is the text for a course in the subject area Missions. This course is designed for 5 hours of group study. Credit is awarded for attending class sessions and reading the book. A person who is absent from one or more class sessions must complete the Personal Learning Activities for the material missed.

Credit also is allowed for use of this material in individual study and, if so designated, in lesson course study and in institutional study.

A person desiring credit for individual study should read this book and complete the Personal Learning Activities.

Credit for this study can be applied to one or more diplomas in the Church Study Course.

After the course is completed, the teacher, the study course clerk, the learner, or any person designated by the church should complete Form 151 (Church Study Course Credit Request, Revised 1975) and send it to the Awards Office, 127 Ninth Avenue, North, Nashville, Tennessee 37234.